ISSUE 3, JULY 2018

AUSTRALIAN FOREIGN AFFAIRS

T0363058

Contributors

Endy M. Bayuni is a senior editor of *The Jakarta Post* and has reported on Indonesia–Australia relations since 1984.

Tim Harcourt is a fellow at the University of New South Wales and a former chief economist of Austrade, the ACTU and the Reserve Bank of Australia.

John Keane is the professor of politics at the University of Sydney and the author of *The Life and Death of Democracy*.

Tim Lindsey is a professor of Asian law and the director of the Centre for Indonesian Law, Islam and Society at the University of Melbourne.

Richard McGregor is a senior fellow for East Asia at the Lowy Institute, and the author of two books on China, *The Party* and *Asia's Reckoning*.

Jennifer Rayner is an economic policy adviser and a former youth ambassador to Indonesia who holds a PhD from the Australian National University.

Ric Smith has served as Australian ambassador to Indonesia, secretary of the defence department and special envoy for Afghanistan and Pakistan.

Jenny Town is the managing editor of 38 North and research analyst at the Stimson Center in Washington.

Julia Wallace is a journalist based in Phnom Penh and a former executive editor of *The Cambodia Daily*.

Hugh White is a professor of strategic studies at the Australian National University and a former deputy secretary in the defence department.

Australian Foreign Affairs is published three times a year by Schwartz Publishing Pty Ltd. Publisher: Morry Schwartz. ISBN 978-1-76064-0675 ISSN 2208-5912 ALL RIGHTS RESERVED. No part of this publication may be reproduced, stored in a retrieval system, or transmitted in any form by any means, electronic, mechanical, photocopying, recording or otherwise, without the prior consent of the publishers. Essays, reviews and correspondence © retained by the authors. Subscriptions – 1 year print & digital auto-renew (3 issues): $49.99 within Australia incl. GST. 1 year print and digital subscription (3 issues): $59.99 within Australia incl. GST. 2 years print & digital (6 issues): $114.99 within Australia incl. GST. 1 year digital only: $29.99. Payment may be made by MasterCard, Visa or Amex, or by cheque made out to Schwartz Publishing Pty Ltd. Payment includes postage and handling. To subscribe, fill out and post the subscription card or form inside this issue, or subscribe online: www.australianforeignaffairs. com or subscribe@australianforeignaffairs.com Phone: 1800 077 514 or 61 3 9486 0288. Correspondence should be addressed to: The Editor, Australian Foreign Affairs, Level 1, 221 Drummond Street, Carlton VIC 3053 Australia Phone: 61 3 9486 0288 / Fax: 61 3 9486 0244 Email: enquiries@australianforeignaffairs.com Editor: Jonathan Pearlman. Associate Editor: Chris Feik. Consulting Editor: Allan Gyngell. Deputy Editor: Julia Carlomagno. Editorial Intern: Ebony Young. Management: Caitlin Yates. Marketing: Elisabeth Young and Georgia Mill. Publicity: Anna Lensky. Design: Peter Long. Production Coordination: Hanako Smith. Typesetting: Tristan Main. Cover portrait of Joko Widodo © Adam Ferguson. Printed in Australia by McPherson's Printing Group.

AUSTRALIA & INDONESIA

Every day in Australia, about thirty-seven flights go to Auckland and thirty-four to Singapore, but just two – sometimes three, depending on the day – fly to Jakarta. More people travel to Ho Chi Minh City, to Vancouver or to Johannesburg each year than to the capital of our largest northern neighbour.

This may seem a crude measure of the relationship between Australia and Indonesia, but other statistics are just as revealing. Last year, Australia conducted more trade with Hong Kong (population 7 million, world's 34th-largest economy) than with Indonesia (population 260 million, world's 16th-largest economy). Indonesian language study at Australian universities has declined, and there has been no increase in Indonesian students coming to Australia in the past twenty years, despite a fivefold overall surge in international enrolments.

This hardly fits the neighbourly vision outlined by successive modern Australian leaders.

The rhetoric has been memorable, ranging from "no country is more important" (Paul Keating) to "more Jakarta, less Geneva" (Tony Abbott). But diplomatic, economic and cultural relations remain marred by mistrust and ignorance, which are difficult to combat in the face of what often seems like deep indifference. The people and governments of both nations appear to be ignoring the warning that intimate and lasting ties are not a "take-it-or-leave-it affair" (Keating again).

Perhaps the most incredible aspect of Australia's relationship with Indonesia is not that it has gone backwards from a very low base, but that these two nations, despite their proximity, have successfully made themselves so invisible to each other.

It is quite a feat, and it leaves both nations poorer. Ultimately it will matter more to Australia than to Indonesia, which is the world's fourth-most populous country and most populous Islamic-majority nation, and is becoming one of the world's strongest economies. Australia needs to do it all it can to develop ties with Indonesia now, because the task could soon become more difficult.

Australia's global economic weight is likely to shrink over time, and its military edge in the Asia-Pacific region is already fading. Furthermore, the status and allure that Australia gains from being a close ally of the region's dominant player, the United States, will diminish as China rises and Beijing challenges Washington's primacy in Asia.

All of this occurs as Indonesia moves away from liberalism and tolerance. Sadly, its democratic tide appears to have peaked, which could put further strain on its relations with Australia.

For now, there are few exceptions to this mutual invisibility. The two nations have developed close military and police links, particularly in countering terrorism and in responding to humanitarian disasters, but this will not be enough to sustain a deep or lasting relationship.

The other exception is Bali, Australia's sixth-most-popular foreign destination (about 20 flights a day land in Denpasar). But it too often proves the rule. As former Indonesian president Susilo Bambang Yudhoyono told Australia's parliament in 2010: "Indonesia is a beautiful archipelago, but we are infinitely more than a beach playground with coconut trees."

To address this great ignorance and indifference, both nations will need to change their perceptions of each other. At present, too little, aside from geography, is keeping them close.

Jonathan Pearlman

THE JAKARTA SWITCH

Why Australia needs to pin its hopes
(not fears) on a great and powerful Indonesia

Hugh White

The arithmetic is clear: if Indonesia can keep growing around 5 per cent a year for the next two or three decades, as it has done so far this century, it will become the world's fifth-largest economy by 2040, and the fourth-largest by 2050; in sheer economic weight it will come in behind only China, India and the United States. Already by 2030 – when Australia's new submarines may just be starting to enter service – its GDP will be three times Australia's, and almost as big as Japan's. Wealth is the ultimate foundation of national power, so that will make Indonesia, or *should* make Indonesia, a very powerful country. It will have the material resources to be a great power in Asia, able to exercise major influence over affairs not just in its immediate neighbourhood but also throughout our region. And it has the potential to be far more important to Australia than we have ever conceived.

It may even become as important to us as China, because while it will not match China's wealth and power, it is much closer – and that could make all the difference. Never underestimate the importance of proximity.

And yet nothing about Indonesia today presages this. It hardly seems a country poised to become a great power and an arbiter of strategic affairs. On the contrary, it appears to be drifting along pretty much as it has for decades: a large, diverse, complex, self-absorbed and rather shambolic nation that still punches way below its weight on the regional stage, and barely registers globally. It seems little able to make sense of the power it is steadily accruing as its economy grows, or of how to use this power. Here, then, is the paradox of Indonesia's position in Asia today: economic growth is driving it towards a position of political and economic influence that it seems both uninterested in and incapable of exploiting.

To some in Australia this may sound like good news. The argument goes that the less Indonesia can turn its increasing economic weight into effective strategic power, the better. That's understandable, because we have got used to thinking that we have more to fear than to hope for from our large neighbour. For much of the seventy-five years since it emerged, rather unexpectedly, as a vast new state on our doorstep, Indonesia has appeared more as a liability than an asset on Australia's strategic balance sheet. At first, Sukarno's unsettling brand of assertive nationalism raised credible fears both that Indonesia could threaten us directly and that it could offer more distant hostile powers access to territory close to our shores. It mostly looked a lot less threatening under Suharto's New Order, which lasted from 1967 to 1998, but the potential for conflict never disappeared. Indeed, after Australia's retreat from Vietnam and until very recently, the possibility of conflict with Indonesia remained the principal focus of our defence policy, even though – despite recurring tensions over East Timor and West Papua – the risk has mostly been very remote.

Moreover, this perception of Indonesia as a potential danger has not been offset by any real sense that it could also be a major strategic asset to Australia, helping to shield us from more-distant threats. That is because we have been so confident that such threats could not arise while the United States continued to exercise clear and uncontested strategic leadership in Asia; it has been easy to overlook Indonesia's potential to help defend us as long as America's power, which has kept the region so stable and peaceful for so long, seemed unassailable.

Indonesia's potential as an ally is more important to us now than it has ever been

Some have long understood Indonesia's potential as a strategic asset for Australia. As the Dibb Review, a survey of Australia's defence capacities, put it back in 1986, Indonesia "forms a protective barrier to Australia's northern approaches"; the review emphasised our shared interest in keeping our neighbourhood "free from interference by potentially hostile external powers". This reflects the simple fact that just as Indonesia is the only close neighbour strong enough to pose any serious threat to us, so too is it the only one strong enough to help us resist the intrusion of a potential adversary to within striking range of our shores. And proximity means the two countries' interests naturally align: a threat to one by a major external power must also threaten the other. This does not guarantee that Australia's and Indonesia's interests and objectives will always coincide in the face of a threat from outside our shared neighbourhood, but it does mean that such alignment is inherently more likely for Australia than with any other Asian major or middle power. Just as our closeness with Indonesia gives us many reasons or pretexts to be enemies, it also gives as many reasons to become allies. And this means that Indonesia's growing power can be both good and bad news for Australia, making it both a more valuable potential ally and a more dangerous potential adversary.

But its potential as an ally is swiftly becoming more important to us as the wider order in Asia shifts. While the United States remained the region's dominant power we had nothing to fear from any state except Indonesia, but now we face a very different region in which America's position is much weaker, and China's, in particular, is much stronger. The central challenge for Australia's foreign policy in the decades ahead will be to manage China's growing power and influence, and to prevent it becoming a threat to us while maximising our independence and freedom of manoeuvre. Indonesia could be a critical ally for us in achieving that goal, quite possibly the most important ally we would have. And the more powerful it becomes and the more effectively it learns to use its power, the more help to us it can be. So while we can never ignore Indonesia's potential as a threat, its potential as an ally is more important to us now than it has ever been, and will become more important still over the decades ahead. That means we in Australia should hope that it can indeed realise its potential as a major power, and make sense of that power to use it effectively. And it means we need to understand much better than we do now how likely that is to happen, and how events will unfold if it does.

Can Indonesia grow despite itself?

First question: will Indonesia's economic arithmetic work out? Can it, as the predictions I opened with presuppose, keep growing for the next few decades as fast as it has for the last two? In some ways it will be surprising if it does, because Indonesia ticks so few of the boxes assumed to be required for sustained growth. Infrastructure is poor, the legal system is weak, protectionist impulses are strong, political favouritism is rampant and corruption remains untamed. These problems could all be fixed, but only by a government able to make tough decisions and overrule vested interests. Alas, Indonesia does not have that kind of government. The political system that has evolved since Suharto's New Order collapsed in 1998 is genuinely democratic, open and competitive. But power is now so widely distributed, and competition for it is so vigorous, that no one from the president down has enough clout by themselves, or can marshal enough support from others, to make vital reforms stick. In a word, Indonesia's government is weak.

And yet despite its shortcomings, Indonesia has managed to grow steadily ever since it recovered from the Asian financial crisis of the late 1990s. It has averaged only slightly slower growth than Vietnam, which is often seen as a model of strong government and effective policy. So maybe we should rethink our assumptions about growth. Until now it has appeared that strong, effective, even ruthless government is essential to sustained economic growth, as the experience of the famous Asian tigers Singapore, Taiwan and South Korea – not to mention China – seems to affirm. Perhaps it remains true that this kind of government is necessary for very fast growth – the 10 per cent per annum rates that the tigers have all managed for long periods. But in today's world it seems that slower but still strong growth can be sustained by countries without the formidably focused and effective state machinery of the tigers. The most important example of this is India. Like Indonesia, it has a weak government unable to achieve the reforms needed if it is to follow the example of the Asian tigers. But it too has managed to grow strongly, if much more erratically than Indonesia, and everyone seems to assume that it will keep growing to take its place behind China as the world's second-largest economy.

So it may be that, in a more globalised world economy, external circumstances count more than they did, and internal ones correspondingly less, in setting the preconditions for fast growth. If so, we should prudently expect Indonesia to keep growing steadily as long as those external circumstances remain reasonably favourable, with no major economic or strategic disasters.

A nation in need of an outlook

But this is only half the story. The other half concerns what Indonesia might do with its wealth and power if and as it grows. This is hard to judge because Indonesia, over its short history, has not developed any clearly discernible conception of itself as an international actor. Indeed, compared to neighbours such as Singapore, Thailand, Vietnam or the Philippines – or Australia – it still has a curiously elusive strategic personality. Its first two decades, under Sukarno, were dominated by the struggle for independence from the Dutch, trying to hold the new republic together and attempting to keep free from Cold War rivalry. This led Sukarno and his colleagues to

Indonesia still has a curiously elusive strategic personality

project a leading role for Indonesia among what he called the New Emerging Forces of the postcolonial world – the new nation-states of Asia and Africa – and a distinctly assertive approach to what he saw as the residual vestiges of colonialism. As part of this, he and his colleagues articulated two ideas – an "independent and active" foreign policy and non-alignment – that have remained central to the way Indonesia talks of its international relations. These ideas reflected, above all, a determination to avoid intrusion by other countries, especially great powers, into Indonesia's internal affairs, and Indonesian entanglement in rivalries between other countries. The aim was to not have its policies dictated by anyone. These principles have endured as foundational to Indonesian foreign policy, remaining central to the nation's view of itself and its international objectives to this day.

But almost everything else changed after 1965, when Sukarno's highly assertive "living dangerously" foreign policy was replaced by Suharto's much more modest, even self-effacing approach. Membership in ASEAN – a regional grouping Indonesia helped to form in 1967, initially to promote stability and reduce the threat of communist insurgencies – became the centrepiece of Indonesia's foreign policy. ASEAN's precepts of non-interference and non-alignment gelled with Indonesia's priorities, but it also provided a setting in which Indonesia could abstain from any attempt to shape the region around it, except in close coordination with its smaller neighbours. This worked fine for Suharto: it allowed him to build friendly and trusting relations with neighbours, while saving his government's energy and attention for internal security and economic development. But in return Indonesia had to accept that it was punching far below its weight in regional affairs. That worked for Indonesia because Suharto's long rule coincided with an unusually stable and peaceful era in Asia. After Nixon's opening to China in 1972, and despite its failure in Vietnam, the United States emerged as Asia's uncontested dominant power. The last vestiges of colonialism were swept away, and Cold War ideological and strategic rivalries faded as America's position became unassailable. Washington was happy to leave Indonesia to follow its own path, and US primacy ensured that no other great power had a chance to interfere seriously in Indonesian affairs, let alone threaten it directly.

Comfortably placed like this, and made doubly secure by its size and location, Indonesia didn't really need a foreign policy for much of the Suharto era, and it didn't really have one beyond the commitment to work within ASEAN.

And nothing much changed in the *Reformasi* era that followed the New Order after Suharto fell in 1998. Over the years that came after, leaders in Indonesia, as elsewhere, took it for granted that America's preponderance globally and in Asia was assured for as far ahead as it was possible to see. The promise of the "Asian Century", underpinned by US power and guided by an expanded ASEAN, seemed to assure Indonesian political and policy elites that no significant change in the New Order's approach was needed. This suited the character of the presidents who came to power under *Reformasi*. Abdurrahman Wahid, Megawati Sukarnoputri and Susilo Bambang Yudhoyono (SBY) were all somewhat self-effacing, and happy enough to maintain Indonesia's low profile and modest diplomatic and strategic agenda. SBY was perhaps more ambitious than his predecessors, seeking to expand Indonesia's international horizons and influence, travelling widely and engaging on issues far removed from Indonesia's backyard. But it was hard to see a clear policy agenda or coherent objectives in his peregrinations. He evidently had a sense of Indonesia's growing power, but lacked a clear idea of how or why to use it, as can be seen in his favourite description of his foreign policy: forging "a million friends and zero enemies".

At first it seemed that SBY's successor, current president Joko Widodo ("Jokowi"), might be different. He is the first president from a new political generation without roots in the Suharto years. He came to office with few ties to Jakarta's political establishment, and his total lack of foreign policy experience meant that he had no personal or political investment in the orthodox Jakarta policy consensus. His election platform had a distinctly nationalist tinge, as did that of his main opponent, the ex-general Prabowo Subianto. The impression that Jokowi represented a more confident, ambitious and assertive Indonesia was apparently confirmed soon after his election, when he attended the G20 summit in Brisbane in 2014. As the leaders assembled, Jokowi reportedly moved from his assigned place to take a seat among the larger powers, remarking that this is where Indonesia, as a big country, *negara besar*, belonged.

More substantively, in 2014 Jokowi launched a significant initiative to redefine Indonesia's profile and posture, positing the idea of Indonesia as a "global maritime fulcrum". This phrase – likely as opaque in Bahasa Indonesia as it is in English – was intended to cover several policy initiatives, both domestic and international, but the key element was to establish Indonesia's position as a major maritime power able to defend its vast archipelago, contribute to the security of the vital trade routes that pass by and through it, and exercise strategic weight in the wider maritime domain beyond it. This at last looked like Indonesia stepping up to take its place in the region, not just as a member of ASEAN but as a significant power in its own right. But that is not how things have played out. Nothing much has come of the global maritime fulcrum idea except some rearrangement of bureaucratic deckchairs in Jakarta. And while in his early days there were other signs that Jokowi intended to forge a new path for Indonesia in which ASEAN was less central, and which focused more on promoting Indonesia's economic and security interests, little has come of this so far, as his first term draws to a close. The continuities in his foreign policy have been much more pronounced than the innovations.

Challenges in the new Asia

This is a problem for Indonesia: its foreign policy remains frozen in postures that worked well in decades past but are less and less suited to the region it faces today. Like all of us in East Asia,

Indonesia faces a massive challenge in adapting to the transformation of Asia's strategic order

Indonesia faces a massive challenge in adapting to the transformation of Asia's strategic order, which is being driven by China and its now plainly evident ambition to become the region's leading power. Although Indonesia has never been a US ally – Indonesia may have no treaty assurances that America will come to its aid if attacked – it has still benefited enormously from America's strategic leadership in Asia, because the stability and order that US power has imposed for so long have virtually guaranteed that Indonesia faces no serious military threat to its territorial security. And while there have been serious differences between Jakarta and Washington over several major issues, including East Timor, Jakarta could and did assume that America posed no serious threat to Indonesia's core interests. Seen from Jakarta, the United States has been a benign regional hegemon.

This has meant that Indonesia has had no need to do much, if anything, to defend itself, or to try to shape the region to prevent threats emerging. The situation has allowed Indonesia to keep its defence budget very low – less than 1 per cent of GDP – for decades, and to devote by far the biggest slice of that to the army, which has been designed and used almost entirely for internal security operations. Indonesia, despite occupying the world's largest archipelago, has air and naval forces significantly weaker than tiny Singapore's, or nearby Australia's. Indonesia's navy has only two submarines in service, with another three on the way; a surface fleet of a dozen mostly small, poorly protected warships; and a modest and ill-assorted collection of fighter planes. It is in no position to confront China's swiftly growing naval and air power.

But now that Indonesia, like Australia, faces the awkward reality that the era of American leadership in Asia is fast drawing to a close, and that we are confronting a new and very unfamiliar future, some important points are already clear. China will overtake the United States to become the world's largest economy by a wide margin. It will become much more powerful than any Asian country has been since the rise of the West 250 years ago. It will wield more influence in East Asia than any Asian country since Imperial Japan at its height, seventy-five years ago. America's relative power in the region will be less than at any time since it won the Philippines from Spain in 1898. All this constitutes the most radical change in Asia's strategic order since the end of World War II and the collapse of colonial empires that followed so swiftly. That means it is the most radical shift in Indonesia's strategic surrounds since the colony declared independence in 1945. And it means that Indonesia faces fundamental choices about how to respond. It must decide how to sustain its security when it can no longer rely on US power to preserve order in the region, and how to manage relations with China, avoiding falling too far under China's sway as China tries to take America's place. Every country in Asia faces these choices, and we can recognise in Indonesia's situation many features in common with our own in Australia, which is caught between the increasingly incompatible interests of its closest ally, the United States, and its largest trading partner, China. But no two countries face exactly the same choices because each country's options and priorities are framed by its unique circumstances. Indonesia's choices are especially complex, and especially significant to its neighbours.

Non-alignment is no longer a choice

Indonesia has a difficult history with China. Under Sukarno, the two countries were quite close, working together with others to found the Non-Aligned Movement (a group of states not formally aligned with or against any major power bloc) in the mid-1950s. But relations were severed in 1965 after the failed coup – which Jakarta believed was led by the Indonesian communist party, backed by Beijing – and they were not restored until 1990. The relationship has always been complicated by ambivalence within Indonesia towards its large and influential ethnic Chinese minority. And much like everyone else in Asia, Indonesians worry about China becoming too powerful and throwing its weight around, especially in ways that intrude into Indonesia's internal affairs or impede its freedom of diplomatic manoeuvre. No one wants to live under China's thumb. But at the same time Indonesia has come to see China's importance as a trading partner and investor. China has risen to become the nation's largest export market, and Indonesia has been happy to sign on to big projects under China's Belt and Road infrastructure plan. So it has struggled to find a balance between engaging with China economically and keeping its distance strategically, just as Australia has done.

But of course Indonesia is even closer to the action than Australia, and its uncertain balancing act has been most vividly on show over the South China Sea. China does not contest Indonesian sovereignty over the Natuna Islands, but it does contest Indonesia's maritime claims around them, some of which fall within China's controversial Nine-Dash Line. Nevertheless, for a long time Jakarta sought to stand back from the wider disputes between other ASEAN members and Beijing, presenting itself as an honest broker between them. But since 2016 incidents over fishing rights in the disputed waters have raised the temperature and prompted Jakarta to make a series of gestures to reaffirm its claims and its determination to defend the islands, including upgrading Indonesia's modest military facilities there.

Some in Washington have eagerly read this as evidence of Indonesia's willingness to align more closely with America in its efforts to push back against China's regional ambitions, a theme US Defense Secretary Jim Mattis emphasised on a visit to Jakarta in January this year. But that seems very unlikely. Indonesia would certainly welcome a continued strong US role in Asia to balance and limit China's power and influence, but like many others – including Australia – it will be very reluctant to take any steps that could risk a serious backlash from China. This means it will likely do nothing material to support the United States against China, despite its anxieties. That seems even clearer since Donald Trump's announcement late last year that the US

The big choice Indonesia faces today... is what to do as US power in Asia dwindles

embassy in Israel would move to Jerusalem, a move that caused anger in Muslim-majority Indonesia and earned a swift public denunciation from Jokowi. More fundamentally, however, overtly siding with the United States against China would make no sense at all unless the United States had both the capacity and the resolve to resist China's challenge effectively – and that is far from clear. No one plans to back a probable loser.

As well, of course, supporting the United States over China would go against Indonesia's deeply held principle of non-alignment. Consistent with that, some Indonesian figures have spoken of

Indonesia again seeking an "honest broker" role, trying to mediate an accord between Washington and Beijing, rather than taking one side against the other. But this too is wishful thinking. There is no place for mediation so long as the two sides' preferred outcomes remain diametrically opposed. A compromise deal is theoretically possible, and would be an excellent outcome, but seems increasingly improbable, and not for lack of mediation. The balance of power and resolve is clearly swinging China's way, America's negotiating position is swiftly eroding, and the scope for it to win any substantive role in Asia's strategic future is narrowing. Hence it is becoming more likely that the United States will eventually, and perhaps not even reluctantly, conclude that the costs of confronting China in Asia are more than the goal is worth, and quietly back away. The big choice Indonesia faces today, therefore, is what to do as US power in Asia dwindles and perhaps disappears, and China steps forth to take America's place.

Options for handling China

How could Indonesia respond to this? One possibility is to do nothing and keep muddling along, armed with the hope that ASEAN will fill the gap as US power in Asia fades. This is fanciful. ASEAN has been very effective in managing relations between its members over the decades when Asia's great powers were held in check by US primacy. But ASEAN is powerless to respond effectively to China's current ambitions because its members cannot reach a consensus about what that response should be. There are good reasons for that: geographical differences alone ensure that Indonesia's views of China, for example, will always be different from Vietnam's. So if Indonesia does nothing over coming decades but muddle along as it has done, it will find itself less able to rely on ASEAN, and without having developed a viable alternative, leaving it increasingly isolated, and increasingly susceptible to Chinese pressure. It will end up, in other words, operating as a minor power in the Asian strategic order, unable to do anything much to shape the region around it or to deflect Chinese pressure on any issue on which Beijing chooses to exert its influence.

This is not by any means an impossible path for Indonesia, but it seems unlikely. Many countries have no choice about being a minor power, as they lack the geographic size and economic weight to be anything more. Indonesia is not one of them. It will have the option, if it chooses, to play an influential role in Asia and to shape the way the region responds to the rise of China as US power fades. It will not have the clout to rival China for East Asian leadership, but it could work with others to keep China's ambitions in check.

One option would be to align with other major Asian powers, most obviously Japan and India, to try to balance China and prevent it becoming the pre-eminent power in East Asia. The agreement for closer defence and strategic cooperation with India announced during Indian Prime Minister Modi's visit to Jakarta in late May is an intriguing hint that Indonesia is starting to think about such possibilities. But there is a long way to go before modest diplomatic set-pieces like this amount to much strategically. That would depend on whether India or Japan are willing to play that role. It is a long shot, especially as Japan and India have such divergent interests in relation to China, both from each other and from Indonesia.

A more credible possibility would be for Indonesia to focus closer to home. Instead of trying to contest China's position in the region as a whole, it could take a more modest path, aiming to limit the influence of China in its own sub-region, in which it could be seen as the natural leading power. That would mean establishing a sphere of influence in maritime South-East Asia, aiming to minimise China's sway by helping its smaller close neighbours to resist Beijing's pressure. It would be a classic "smaller great power" strategy. The advantage of this approach is that Indonesia's interests would naturally align with its neighbours', in trying to minimise China's influence over them – at least as long as Indonesia itself did not become an irksome or threatening local hegemon.

This scenario is made more plausible by the fact that Indonesia and its close neighbours seem likely to find themselves in an advantageous position on the boundary line between a Chinese sphere of influence in the Western Pacific and an Indian sphere of influence in the Indian Ocean. The currently fashionable idea of the "Indo-Pacific region" does not lead us to consider this, because it presupposes that India and China are somehow fated to compete for primacy across the whole mega-system. But that is far from the most likely outcome. Their interests would each be better served by avoiding a direct challenge, so it seems rather more probable that the two strongest powers will agree to divide Asia between them, along the line between the Indian and Pacific oceans. Indonesia, sitting on that line, would have plenty of chances to play the two bigger powers off against each other and maximise its room to manoeuvre between them.

A third possibility for Indonesia, also credible, would be to try to stand alone. Rather than building a local sphere of influence among its close neighbours to keep China (and India) at bay, it could focus more narrowly on maximising its independence by holding aloof from regional power politics but standing ready to defend its own territory and

The old anti-colonial impulses will become less and less helpful in guiding Indonesia

freedom of action. This would be a kind of "armed and neutral" posture, on the model of Switzerland or Sweden, which is a classic middle-power strategy. For Jakarta, it would have the appeal of continuing the preoccupation with non-alignment and independence that has been central to Indonesian thinking about its place in the world since the 1940s.

Recasting Indonesia

None of these potential new postures would be easy. From today's perspective they all look speculative or even fanciful, because they are so far from anything that seems to have been contemplated in Jakarta before. Each would require a fundamental shift in Indonesia's view of itself and its place in the region and the world. In some ways, that view is still framed by the struggle against colonialism, which defined Indonesia's identity at its birth and remains deeply imprinted on its national psyche today. That is perhaps understandable if one sees the US regional leadership of recent decades as a continuation of the Western domination of Asia after the European empires collapsed. But as US power fades, the old anti-colonial impulses will become less and less helpful in guiding Indonesia as it navigates an Asia that, for the first time in many centuries, is in the hands of Asian states themselves. Indonesia has to decide what part it wants to play in a region that will be vastly different from the one it has known since independence, in order to avoid becoming increasingly irrelevant and vulnerable to the power of other nations.

That will require a rethinking of not only Jakarta's diplomatic agenda but also its military power. If Indonesia is to play any significant role in the power politics of Asia over coming decades, it will need to become a substantial maritime power. That is a huge challenge, and the modest steps of recent years, such as the ordering of three new submarines, barely constitute a start. It is a lot to ask of Indonesia's current defence establishment, which appears to lack the vision, the managerial skills and the technical know-how to create the kinds of maritime forces needed to underpin a major regional strategy for Indonesia in the years ahead. Indeed, this would require a radical transformation of the defence organisation and its political leadership. That does not mean it can't be done, but it can't be done easily.

This all reaffirms how hard it is going be for Indonesia to respond effectively to the challenges posed by the transformation of the regional order that is now well underway. It helps to explain why Indonesian political elites have been so reluctant to acknowledge the significance of that transformation: the shift tests the whole nature of the Indonesian state. The reality seems to be that while Indonesia's economy can keep growing despite the weakness of its government system, it cannot harness and apply the power that its growing economy will deliver unless those weaknesses are effectively remedied. And this seems unlikely within the structures and systems that have evolved in Jakarta over the twenty years since *Reformasi* was launched after the fall of Suharto.

Asia, for the first time in many centuries, is in the hands of Asian states

Indonesia will need more than new government leaders. To take its place as a major regional player, it will also need a new stronger system of democratic government – one that is better able to reconcile competing interests, to curb corruption and favouritism, to make hard decisions and to ensure those decisions are implemented effectively.

Can we be friends?

All of this matters a great deal to Australia. Whether Indonesia can emerge as a major power, and, if it can, how it will use its power will have immense implications for us. We still do not see this because, like most Indonesians, we have been slow to understand and acknowledge the scale and significance of the shifts that are transforming our region. As US power wanes, a weak Indonesia drifting more and more into China's orbit would make it much harder for us to avoid the same fate. An Indonesia that is willing and able to articulate and implement a coherent and ambitious foreign policy, and to build the military power to support it – a vision that has for so long been a source of Australian fear – may now be a source of hope, and may need to be actively encouraged. That is because a strong Indonesia determined to maximise its independence from China, and from India, could make it much easier for Australia to maintain our freedom of manoeuvre.

Bringing this about would not just require great changes in Indonesia. It would require great changes here too, because the strategic relationship we might build with a powerful and influential Indonesia would be quite different from any we have known before. Until now we have had only two kinds of key strategic relationships: our close alliances with our two great and powerful Anglo-Saxon friends have been all about dependence and subordination; and through our defence cooperation programs we have been the strategic patron of what used to be weaker and less advanced neighbours in

South-East Asia, offering a helping hand from a position of superiority. A successful relationship with a powerful Indonesia would look nothing like either of these. We would not be in any sense the senior partner in such a relationship, but neither could we be the subordinate – we could never afford simply to depend on Indonesia as we have on Britain and the United States, so the relationship we might build would not resemble the kind of closely intertwined alliances we have known with them for so long. It would have to be an equal partnership between unequal partners, whose interests clearly converge but will not always coincide. Such relationships are common enough in history – think of America and Britain for much of the twentieth century –

A strong Indonesia that shares Australia's aims would be an immense asset

but unprecedented for Australia, so we have a lot to learn about how to make them work.

It is far from clear whether there is much Australia can do to nudge Indonesia towards taking on the kind of active and effective role that would serve our interests, but there are practical things the two nations could do together to build their capability to play such roles, and enhance the scope for cooperation in so doing – for example, by helping one another build modern air and naval forces and maritime surveillance capabilities. There would always be limits to this cooperation, because the old dilemma would never disappear.

A strong Indonesia that shares Australia's aims would be an immense asset, while one that is hostile to Australia could pose unprecedented threats. Which of these possibilities might emerge may well matter more to our strategic future than anything else. It is no one's responsibility but ours to ensure that, in the Asian Century, Indonesia is indeed an asset to us, and not a liability. But one would hardly know it from the way we think about Indonesia and deal with it today. ■

THE VIEW FROM AUSTRALIA

Is Indonesia leaving
us behind?

Jennifer Rayner

"Flares, flares everywhere, in the flatland darkness, where gabled villas with orange-tiled roofs hid behind crumbling walls, and a dark, drain-like canal moved with evil slowness. On an area of muddy ground beside the highway, the lights from the pasar *[market] burned uncertainly: kerosene and gas pressure-lamps set on the counters of many little stalls under tattered awnings … All the brown faces, floating in flatland dark, were theatrically lit from below, by the brazier, by the flares; and all seemed to smile. Young men in white shirts and sarongs walked by hand in hand. Doorless huts gave glimpses of public privacy, frozen in yellow frames: a table with a candle on it; a small, naked girl playing on a straw mat; a middle-aged woman in a sarong and incongruous brassière, heating water in a discarded can over a little fire. The rooms were so small they were little more than boxes, and could not be stood up in: children's playhouses."*

This is Jakarta as described by C.J. Koch in *The Year of Living Dangerously*, the most (read: only) well-known Australian book about Indonesia. Koch was writing in 1978 – a time when political tempers and the country's economy were badly fraying, not yet even halfway through then president Suharto's long years of autocracy.

Forty years on, and to the extent that Indonesia features in the Australian imagination at all, it is still largely as Koch described it. A poor, hot and hardscrabble place, bedevilled by corruption, beset by violence and natural disaster; a nation of skinny brown foster children who reach out to us with needy hands. According to a poll conducted last year by the Lowy Institute, less than a third of us are even aware it is a democracy.

We couldn't be more wrong.

Indonesia is very likely Asia's next big power, another engine of growth that will drag the pole of the world's economy ever more strongly towards our region. The rise of the Chinese and Indian economies has overshadowed its rapid blooming of wealth, but it has come too far, too fast now, to be ignored.

Australia is not just ill equipped to deal with this scenario; we don't really even *see* it. We imagine ourselves as the neighbourhood's rich benefactors, chucking change to the poor kids while keeping our distance in case they start asking too much of us.

But Indonesia's rise means our current situation has more in common with the residents of a highway country town when a bypass is going in: there's a real risk all the action is going to pass us by.

This is because Indonesia does not really need Australia today, and will need us even less in the decades ahead as its wealth and power continue to grow. In engaging with this country, we currently have little of the leverage to call upon that strengthens our other major economic relationships: neither the bonds of history nor the demand for our goods.

If we do not make an effort with Indonesia, there is a risk that it will simply look straight past us, to partners elsewhere in the region and beyond. Far from asking too much of us, we will instead be irrelevant to its progress and bystanders to its prosperity. That would be a grievously missed opportunity for Australia as we look to diversify our economy away from China and protect our own affluence in the years to come.

That effort starts with lifting our noses out of Koch's pages, and seeing Indonesia as it is today.

The Qantas flight from Sydney to Jakarta gets you in at dusk, when the sky is turning pinky-orange, and traffic haze, charcoal smoke and the keening call to prayer smudge the hard edges off everything. It's the worst time of day to join the packed elevated highways that swoop from the airport into the business district, unless the city's famous *macet* – the terrible congestion that plagues central Jakarta – is what you've come to see.

As I drove in on my last trip with a first-time visitor who'd trailed me over there, his astonishment as Jakarta sprawled out before us bordered on comic. Twisting and turning in his seat to take in more of the skyscrapers and over-bright billboards that spilled out in every direction, he breathed: "It's like a *real* city!"

A real city, for an increasingly rich country.

For Australians, it is a struggle to get our heads around Indonesia as anything but poor and backward. In 2016 the Australia–Indonesia Centre at Monash University undertook a major survey to understand the perceptions people in these two countries have about ourselves and each other. The study found that while Indonesians are extremely optimistic about their economic fortunes and prospects, less than one in five of the Australians surveyed believe that the country is prosperous or has a strong economy. Highlighting the deep scars of the Bali and Jakarta embassy bombings, there were more Australian participants who perceived Indonesia to be an unsafe place than there were who viewed it as an important trading partner for us. And while people in both countries expressed an interest in developing closer relations, Australians saw the advantages of this primarily in terms of cultural exchange and tourism, not hard economics.

So far, so predictable: many Australians don't think much about Indonesia except as a cheap place for a beachside holiday. But the survey also contained a telling finding about the way Indonesians perceive us, one that should hover over our thinking about the relationship from here. Fully 70 per cent of Indonesians now believe their country is more important to Australia than ours is to them.

We've known this was coming – in 2015 *The Jakarta Post* published an editorial whose headline gave blunt advice: "Australia needs to figure out its own place in Asia". One of its authors was a former ambassador to this country; the other was a journalist (and contributor to this publication) who knows both nations well. They argued that our politicians should stop trying to make Indonesia Australia's most important relationship because:

> not only does it make no difference to Indonesia, but it also makes us uncomfortable, since we can never reciprocate the feeling. Australia is barely in the top five of Indonesia's most important relationships; some may even say that it would be lucky to be in the top 10.

It's probably fortunate hardly anyone in Australia reads the Indonesian press; there wouldn't have been enough icepacks in the country to soothe this sick burn to our national ego otherwise.

Of course, Indonesia has long applied a certain belligerence and swagger to its international engagements, going right back to former president Sukarno's role in mustering small Asian and African states into the Non-Aligned Movement as an up-yours to Western powers in the 1950s. But Indonesia's current confidence and assertiveness is backed up by an important economic shift: it is now almost as rich as we are in absolute terms, and on track to get much richer.

Scoff if you like, but here are the numbers. In 1998, when Indonesia's democratic era began, the country's GDP was just a quarter of Australia's. Twenty years later, Indonesia is fast closing in on us, with its 2016 GDP more than three-quarters of Australia's. Over those years it has bounded from thirty-sixth in the world to sixteenth in total GDP terms, just three places behind Australia. It is expected to leapfrog us to join the world's top ten sometime between 2020 and 2030, depending on which projections you favour.

By way of comparison, Indonesia's 2016 GDP was larger than Singapore's, Thailand's and New Zealand's *combined* – three countries that are in our top ten trading partners, while Indonesia isn't. Although no one would suggest the average Indonesian yet enjoys the wealth or quality of life Australians do, the country's per capita GDP is almost double India's, and has risen by 65 per cent over the past decade.

Like China, Indonesia has been making huge strides in winching people out of poverty. At the turn of the century only about 20 per cent of its citizens belonged to the middle class; by 2010 this had surged to more than 56 per cent. Tens of millions more Indonesians are projected to join their ranks by this century's midpoint. I used to laugh when my work colleagues in Jakarta suggested meeting up at Starbucks; Indonesia produces famously good coffee, and cups of it can be had in cafés across the city for less than a fifth of the price of the chain's foamy, filthy muck. Yet since 2002 Starbucks has opened 326 stores in twenty-two cities across the country, and they are positively thriving, as the mermaid logo becomes an accessible sign of conspicuous consumption for a growing group of the comfortably off.

Indonesia's vast reduction in poverty has come about because the country's economy has been consistently growing by 5 to 6 per cent a year – well above the less than 3 per cent growth we've managed in Australia since the end of the mining boom. Something that will help sustain Indonesia's growth at this rate and move even more people into the middle class is the fact that just over 50 per cent of its current population is under thirty. This gives it a pool of fit and healthy workers that other Asian countries facing exploding dependency ratios and the ballooning costs of ageing, such as Japan, can only envy.

So Indonesia is already on its way to wealth, and getting richer all the time; it's growing strongly, while growth remains lacklustre elsewhere; and it's young, in a

> **We will need to ditch the arrogance and replace it with respect**

region where many of the other big players are ageing. Little wonder, then, that more than three-quarters of those Indonesians participating in that Australia–Indonesia Centre survey expected the country's prosperity and their own standard of living to improve in the next ten years.

Australia cannot properly move forward in its relationship with Indonesia until we acknowledge how far it has come, and how this changes the balance of power we've imagined exists between us. If Australia is not the rich benefactor or the aspirational example we've long seen ourselves to be, then who, exactly, are we to Indonesia today?

Working out a different kind of relationship with Indonesia will require recalibrating our attitudes and approach. We will need to ditch the arrogance – both individually and as a nation – that too often characterises our contact with the country, and replace it with respect.

This recalibration is an important step, but only the first in making sure we don't miss out on the opportunities created by a more affluent Indonesia. At different times Australia has worked hard to improve security ties with Indonesia, but this narrow sphere of cooperation, no matter how vital, has been limited to the elimination of threats and the maintenance of a stable status quo in our Asia-Pacific region. The pursuit of opportunities and the expansion of wealth through greater understanding between our two nations has largely been put off to some future time that never seems to arrive.

Once we start viewing Indonesia as a serious business prospect, it becomes clear just how far behind Australia is in turning the opportunity into reality. Properly doing business with Indonesia demands a set of tools Australia doesn't currently have, and has shown scant interest in acquiring up to now.

It's well acknowledged that the economic relationship between Indonesia and Australia is not what it could be. Despite our proximity, we are not in each other's top ten trading partners and never have been. Our northern neighbour trades more with Japan and the Netherlands – two countries with which it has fought bitter wars within some of its citizens' lifetimes – than it does with us.

But to see just how underdone our current relationship is, consider New Zealand. Australian companies have more than $106 billion invested across the ditch, in a country with a population of under 5 million. On the other hand, Australia's total private investment in Indonesia is estimated at less than $10 billion, despite Indonesia's population being about fifty-five times larger.

The shallowness of our economic relationship is often put down to politics. As Indonesia analyst Ken Ward lays out in his thoughtful book *Condemned to Crisis?*, the diplomatic engagement between Australia and Indonesia has been characterised by long periods of inattention interspersed with flare-ups on issues such as East Timor, asylum seekers and the treatment of Australians who get themselves into trouble in Bali. He notes:

> Clashes of national interests between Australia and Indonesia sparking diplomatic tensions have occurred intermittently over the last seven decades, irrespective of which party has been in power in Canberra ... Some of these clashes, or at least their severity and intractability, can be attributed fairly obviously to the proximity of the two countries ... Moreover, as has often been said, there are sharp differences between these two neighbours.

Drawing on earlier analyses by former Australian foreign minister Gareth Evans and former diplomat Bruce Grant, Ward suggests these differences encompass such minor details as "language, culture, religion, history, population size and ... political, legal and social systems".

There's no doubt the waxing and waning of our political relationship with Indonesia has sometimes undermined the forging of closer economic ties, or that the differences in our histories and institutions can seem stark. But putting it all down to politics lets our companies and policymakers off far too lightly.

A bigger challenge is that Australia's major economic relationships essentially take two forms: we trade with our old friends, and we trade off our natural assets. That sounds glib, but the data bears it out: more than half of our two-way trade currently happens with just five countries. Two of them are our historical allies – the United States and the United Kingdom – and the remaining three are the Asian powerhouses – China, Japan and South Korea – for whom we act as a quarry. In 2016 just under half of all our exports by value comprised bulk commodities, while our top two services exports, education and tourism, made up less than 10 per cent of everything we sold offshore.

Australian governments talk a big game about transitioning to service exports to provide for the rising Asian middle class, and our companies do too. Think of former treasurer Joe Hockey's claim that the "massive change in the demand for services out of the region" will represent "the most transformative event in our history", or ANZ's former CEO Mike Smith touting the "immense" opportunities awaiting Australian business on our northern doorstep. For at least the past decade a succession of trade ministers from Crean to Ciobo have told us the services revolution is moments away, taking us into new markets, securing our prosperity for decades to come.

But still the vast bulk of our trade remains rooted in the lucky accidents of our history and our geomorphic make-up. That simply doesn't get us very far with Indonesia.

The country doesn't need our minerals: it produces almost as much coal as Australia and has huge reserves of gas, gold and other raw materials across its archipelago. Beef, the major agricultural product we currently export there, is the subject of an intensive push by the Indonesian government to achieve self-sufficiency of production within the next ten years.

Australians' lack of interest in learning Bahasa Indonesia is perplexing

And while Australians love Bali's beaches – around a million of us visit each year – Indonesians don't seem to feel the same about our natural attractions, as only around 193,800 Indonesians visited Australia in the last financial year.

As we look to transition to service-led exports, we're also lacking an important asset that helped us at least get a foot in the door of China and India: an Indonesian diaspora. At the 2016 Census, 2.2 per cent of Australians – some 509,555 people – identified as being born in China. Another 1.9 per cent, or 455,389 people, were born in India. Many, many more Aussie-born kids trace ancestry to one of these countries through their parents and grandparents. These people are an enormous asset and resource to Australia as our companies develop products and offerings that can penetrate those big markets, bridging the countries with their language skills and cultural knowledge. By contrast, just 73,213 Indonesian-born people showed up in the census – a bare 0.3 per cent of our population. Only around 65,800 more Australians claim Indonesian ancestry. That leaves us massively short on the human resources needed to deliver the level of economic engagement we've already achieved with countries such as China and India.

So Australia has next to none of the advantages we've leveraged for our existing economic relationships when it comes to doing business with Indonesia. If we want the relationship to grow to its potential, we're going to have to put in a different kind of effort than we have done in the past. Are we willing and able to do that? To be frank, the signs aren't good.

Let's start with the language and cultural competence gap. This is where the divergence between the official rhetoric about the potential of the relationship and any action to deliver on it becomes most obvious, because we're doing bugger all through Australia's schools and universities to make up for our shortfall of Indonesian expertise.

According to a study by the linguist and Asia scholar David Hill, approximately 191,000 students learn some Bahasa Indonesia between kindergarten and Year 12. But almost none of them persist with the language all the way through their school years, which means the feeder pool for university study is incredibly small. Hill found that only a little over 1000 Australian Year 12 students finish school with decent Indonesian language skills – a lower level than in the 1970s. Furthermore, when his report was published in 2012, only fifteen of Australia's forty universities offered standalone Indonesian programs. Between 2004 and 2010, Indonesian programs closed at six Australian universities, including Griffith University and the University of Technology Sydney. In 2012 the University of New South Wales followed suit by announcing the closure of its program, formerly one of the largest in the country.

Hill has suggested that "Australians' preparedness to learn Indonesian language is arguably the most fundamental barometer of the health of the bilateral relationship. It is a quantifiable measure of Australians' interest in, knowledge of, and engagement with Indonesia." By refusing to learn it in anything like decent numbers, we're sending a clear message about how much we *really* value the relationship.

Australians' lack of interest in learning Bahasa Indonesia is particularly perplexing given that, unlike Mandarin or Japanese, mastering it demands no study of complex characters or script, and no ear for tonal nuance. It is entirely possible to become fluent enough to read, write and navigate most social situations with a year's dedicated study. It can only be some combination of laziness and arrogant disinterest that is holding us back. (*Ya, saya bisa bicara bahasa ini. Terima kasih atas pertanyaan Anda.*)[1]

1 Yes, I can speak it. Thanks for asking.

Beyond language, the past few years in domestic debate suggest that Australia may not be ready for our companies to pursue the adaptations necessary to serve a major market very different from our own. The ongoing disquiet over halal certification is the leading example here – recall Pauline Hanson's whine that the Australian production of halal products represents "the Islamisation of Australia", and the claims by politicians such as George Christensen and Jacqui Lambie that the certification fees fund terrorism.

Sure, those are names that readers of a journal such as this might struggle to take seriously. But their silly claims have real consequences. In 2014, for example, the South Australia–based Fleurieu Milk and Yoghurt Company lost a large contract with the airline Emirates after a social media campaign caused it to drop the halal certification of its products. Brands such as Vegemite and Cadbury have been the target of similar public campaigns that received widespread media coverage; in 2015 the Australian Senate even held an inquiry into the halal certification regime and where the money goes, at the instigation of Senator Cory Bernardi. How many of those whipping up this scare are aware, or even care, that halal certification is critical to Australian firms' ability to export into markets like Indonesia? That without it our beef and other products would never make it over the border?

Our lack of maturity regarding this kind of tailoring to foreign markets and cultures makes it harder than it should be for local companies to pursue the opportunities available to them. There are clear service niches that Australian firms *could* explore in Indonesia – Islamic financial services is one that comes to mind, given our banking sector is actively seeking opportunities to grow offshore. But it doesn't take much to imagine the public backlash a brand such as the Commonwealth Bank would cop if it were revealed that the Dollarmites were diversifying into "Sharia banking". This may also help explain why our onshore tourism industry continues to give little thought to amenities and services for Muslim visitors. As just one illustrative example, none of the major national galleries or museums in Canberra signpost facilities for the devout, who need to pray throughout the day.

Indonesia's 260 million consumers are not going to adapt to us; we will need to tailor our services and products to them. If our firms can't do that without getting whacked in their home market, this further shrinks the chances of us making the most of the economic opportunities that are out there.

One more factor that suggests we're not yet in a headspace to truly make this relationship work is the ongoing propensity of Australian governments to take Indonesia by surprise with domestic policy decisions. There have been some very high-profile examples of this, of course: Julia Gillard's snap announcement of a live export ban in 2011; Tony Abbott's unilateral decision to start turning back refugee boats to Indonesian waters in 2014. But this goes on all the time in less prominent ways as well. A recent example was the Australian government's decision to slap anti-dumping duties on Indonesian A4 paper exports in mid-2017, *right in the middle of negotiations between our countries over a new bilateral trade agreement.*

Indonesia's leaders take an extremely dim view of Australia making policy decisions that affect their country without warning or consultation, and they are right to do so. It's inconceivable we would make big decisions that touched China or the United States without engaging them first; those relationships are just too important to us to risk it. Australian policymakers need to get into the habit of asking themselves, "Does this decision affect Indonesia, and how might it react?" as a standard part of the policy development process. We can't keep taking their leaders by surprise and then wondering why trust and goodwill don't flow as easily in this relationship as they do in some of our others.

This is a bit of a chicken-and-egg scenario because Australian governments have little incentive to start factoring the Indonesia relationship into their day-to-day thinking until the economic partnership is larger and more valuable. But it simply won't grow to its potential if every time we take one step forward on economic cooperation, our own blithe thoughtlessness sends us several steps back.

In light of these factors, it seems there are two ways Australia could go from here.

We *could* just accept that we aren't ready or willing to do what it takes to expand our economic reach beyond the familiar, beyond the good fortune that has brought us this far. We could let Indonesia fade out of the discussion about Australia's future prosperity, and get used to living more or less politely as strangers side by side.

Or we could acknowledge that doing what it takes to build a stronger economic relationship with Indonesia will benefit us both in terms of the opportunities that the direct relationship holds *and* in strengthening our capacity to form other beneficial trade relationships in the wider world. Because if we can get Indonesia right, Australia will have made a great step forward in our approach to economic engagement. No more will we be trading only on our lucky breaks.

For me, Indonesia is the noise of motorbikes with busted mufflers that set your teeth on edge as they burn past you down the congested streets. Fried chicken on greaseproof paper bought from a windowed cart; flies competing with ants for your scraps while the chilli blaze of sambal glues the hairs to your neck. The smell of cigarettes and incense and things slowly rotting.

Indonesia is vibrant and complicated, lively and loose

But it's also the ceaseless chirping of a mobile phone in each hand – most office workers I've met carry two. It's malls where the upwardly mobile wander in the scented cool, leather goods worth a week's Australian wage dangling from their arms. It's start-ups and spectacular business deals-then-dust-ups that saturate the pages of the country's many news sites.

Indonesia is vibrant and complicated, lively and loose. You can literally see its wealth rising as new buildings and railway stations sprout up across Jakarta. And you can watch that good fortune roll out across the archipelago in the swathe of port, road and rail projects currently being delivered. It is a place of enormous optimism and potential, a country whose people know its best times are still ahead of it.

Can Australians put aside what we think we know about the place and see Indonesia's rise for the opportunity it is? Can we adapt our approach to trade and try different things that take us beyond our comfort zone? Most importantly, can we come to grips with a new idea of our standing in this relationship and our role in the region's economy?

These are the multi-billion-dollar questions. ■

THE VIEW FROM INDONESIA

Dispatch from an
indifferent neighbour

Endy M. Bayuni

Indonesian and Australian news editors have been gathering together periodically for much of the last twenty years and should – in theory – be able to report truthfully what is happening on the other side. These meetings, funded by the Canberra-based Australia–Indonesia Institute, seek to improve understanding among opinion leaders who could help to encourage the nations to work closely together, as two good neighbours should.

During the introductory round at one such meeting several years ago in Jakarta, some from the Indonesian side revealed that they owned apartments in Sydney, Melbourne, Perth or Brisbane; their Australian counterparts were impressed. A few also said their children were studying in Australia.

Presumably, Indonesian editors must understand Australia pretty well to want to invest money in Australian property, or to entrust their kids to schools or universities there. Yet this apparent affinity for Australia has not been reflected in the way they – and many others in the middle-class elite in Indonesia – discuss the giant neighbour to the south. Nor it is evident in the media reporting on Australia.

Instead, the prevailing view of Australia among Indonesians today has barely changed from the period when Australia had the White Australia Policy in place: just as then, it is seen as racist, arrogant, manipulative, exploitative and intrusive. It is this perception of the old Australia that is particularly evident each time the two nations get into a dispute – and we have had more than our share of those in recent years.

Neighbours can and will disagree. It is the way in which these disagreements are handled that determines the nature of the rela-tionship. And the old, entrenched perceptions of Aussies inevitably make a bad situation worse.

The Indonesian political elite, along with many opinion-makers in the media, know that Australia's population is vastly different to what it was five or six decades ago. The former white colony is now a multi-racial, multi-ethnic and multi-religious nation. Many Asians, and many Muslims, including thousands from Indonesia, have made Australia their home.

But popular perceptions are hard to change, and Indonesians' view of Australia is only shifting slowly. (This is apparently also true of the way Australians see Indonesia: as a poor and backward country, ruled by a military dictator, now veering towards Islamism.) As the popular

Indonesian saying goes, *Tak kenal tak sayang*: you can't love someone if you don't know them. There is still a significant amount of ignorance among the Indonesian public about the new Australia. Love thy neighbour? Perhaps not just yet; not until we know each other better.

With the exception of the middle class, most of Indonesia's 260 million people have had little exposure to Australia, let alone visited it. Trade between our two countries remains slight. There is no obvious Australian icon, a product that is immediately recognisable as Australian in Indonesia. In the 1960s and 1970s, Holden was the vehicle that every elite Jakartan family had in their garage, before Japanese car manufacturers took over the market. No other Australian product or brand name has since taken its place in the Indonesian national imagination. Australian beef may dominate the market, but Indonesia imports the cattle and slaughters it locally, so the beef is sold without Australia's brand attached. Australian wine could be iconic in Indonesia, as it is in some other parts of the world, if Indonesia were not a predominantly Muslim country. (Nonetheless, though only 5 per cent of the population drink, this still represents 13 million people, more than double the population of Singapore.)

So there is little interest among the Indonesian public in what is happening in Australia. Good news doesn't sell, meaning that, for

The Indonesian public has not changed its outdated perceptions of Australia

better or for worse, Australia has been kept out of the media headlines in Indonesia for much of these past few years. Those who might tackle misperceptions have typically found it easier to stay silent, and they risk losing their audience when they speak out. Given this silence, which both reflects and perpetuates the lack of public opinion, it is perhaps not surprising that the Indonesian public, their audience, has not changed its outdated perceptions of Australia and its people.

The recurring pattern of engagement between the two countries is that minor disagreements are allowed to escalate, fuelled by opportunism and stereotypes, which are then reinforced. The good news fades, and so do the prospects for correcting outdated perceptions. It is worth examining precisely how this unfortunate cycle operates, as we can then consider how to reverse it.

The bad news cycle: Bali, boats and beef

Sadly, it is the bad news that still drives the relationship between the two countries. "Bali, boats and beef" are the three Bs that commentators like to single out as defining issues. They will probably remain so for the foreseeable future, given that they have not been resolved. Yet if we look at how these various points of friction developed, it soon becomes clear that much of the strain could have been avoided.

In 2015, the execution of two of the Australian "Bali Nine" drug traffickers, Andrew Chan and Myuran Sukumaran, on President Joko Widodo's orders, set Indonesia and Australia at each other's throats. The Indonesian media, increasingly driven by social media, stoked public anger by reporting that Australia had been campaigning, covertly at first but later openly, for a stay of execution for the two men. The Indonesian media also did little reporting of the fact that the men had repented and even found God during their more than ten years on death row. In a nation that likes to claim to put religion above all else, Indonesians this time put aside compassion, the grounds for Australia's request to spare the men's lives. Instead, they made patriotism and the president's "war on drugs" their foremost concern. They urged the president to carry out the executions to teach Australians a lesson. So much for religion's claims of tolerance and forgiveness.

This dispute was driven by the leaders in both countries. Widodo invoked Indonesia's sovereignty in relation to the men's sentences and denounced Australia's eleventh-hour appeal as Canberra meddling in Jakarta's domestic affairs. Australian prime minister Tony Abbott, desperate to save his two citizens, reminded Indonesia of the A$1 billion in aid that Australia gave after the devastating 2004 tsunami, which followed an earthquake near the northern Indonesian province of Aceh. His foreign minister, Julie Bishop, warned that the execution could hurt Bali's economy, which still depends on sizeable income from Australian tourists.

Both Widodo and Abbott essentially drove the execution plan to its inevitable outcome. The voices of the small band of campaigners against capital punishment in Indonesia were drowned out. The views of those Indonesians who had a strong affinity with Australia, or personal or professional interests there, went virtually unheard – not that their voices would have made much difference, but the absence was glaring.

This has been the pattern throughout many of the disputes that have marked relations between the two countries. There is hardly anyone in Indonesia who would speak up on behalf of Australia, not necessarily to defend it, but to clear up some of the misperceptions the general public have and to counter the disinformation and misinformation that have always clouded these rows. The presence of such a perspective could have prevented the dispute from moving to extremes.

The Australian decision in 2011 to stop exporting beef to Indonesia, a poorly thought-out move that backfired and hurt its own cattle industry more than it did Indonesian consumers, also riled the Indonesian public. Indonesians survived eating less red meat for a short period, but the anti-Australia backlash, including from householders who felt the pinch of the raised beef prices, was harsh. It forced the government to reduce Indonesia's reliance on Australian beef by opening up and encouraging imports from alternative sources, including India.

Indonesians also criticised Australia's decision, under Abbott's leadership, to tow boatloads of asylum seekers back to Indonesian waters, even to the point of Australia buying and equipping them with new boats for the return journey. Unlike in Australia, the fate of "boat people", who are mostly from the Middle East and South Asia, is a minor issue in Indonesia, which is a mere transit point for these asylum seekers. Abbott's decision to go it alone rolled back virtually all the goodwill and cooperation the two governments had built for years in addressing the problem.

One could add a fourth B to the issues that have divided Indonesia and Australia: Bambang. Susilo Bambang Yudhoyono, Indonesia's president from 2004 to 2014, took personal offence at the revelation in 2013 that the Australian government had been eavesdropping on his mobile phone calls, along with those of ten other top Indonesian officials, including his wife. Abbott's evasive response – insisting this was a matter of Australia's national security and not up for public discussion – did not help. Yudhoyono must have felt personally betrayed, for he was the president who took Indonesia's relations with Australia to their historic best. No apology was forthcoming from Canberra, and the matter was left hanging.

Abbott's behaviour can be contrasted with the way former US president Barack Obama handled a similar revelation that the United States had been tapping the telephone of German chancellor Angela Merkel. Although this monitoring had reportedly taken place before Obama's term, he nevertheless apologised, assuring Merkel that an investigation had been undertaken. In the absence of any assurances from Abbott, Indonesian leaders were left with the nagging feeling that Australia would continue to snoop on them. Trust, essential in any relationship, has been thinning since then.

Sources of suspicion: East Timor and Papua

Indonesia and Australia have come a long way from the days in the 1980s and 1990s when East Timor (now Timor-Leste) was the issue that virtually defined their relationship. The former Portuguese territory that Indonesia occupied for more than twenty years stopped becoming – to use the late Indonesian foreign minister Ali Alatas's expression – the "pebble in the shoe" in Indonesia–Australian relations after it seceded in 1999.

Still, the episode left a sour taste for many Indonesian political elites, who even today cannot forgive Australia for prodding then Indonesian president B.J. Habibie's government to allow East Timor to hold a referendum on self-determination. To add insult to injury, after the East Timorese voted overwhelmingly for independence, the United Nations chose Australia to lead the military mission to oversee the transition of power.

Indonesia may have been relieved to let go of East Timor, which, unlike the rest of Indonesia, was not a Dutch colony. Historical scholarship and declassified official documents since then have revealed that Jakarta unwillingly, if not half-heartedly, invaded East Timor in late 1975, with encouragement from Washington and Canberra, which feared the prospect of a leftist government taking over from the departing Portuguese colonial administration. The United States had just lost the war in Vietnam and a Cold War mentality prevailed.

By the 1990s, it was clear that East Timor had become a huge liability, financially as well as politically. Even so, in Jakarta its loss was seen as a betrayal of the thousands of Indonesian soldiers who gave up their lives in seizing and defending the territory. The military and its supporters hold a grudge against Australia for the role it played in bringing about the separation, even though Canberra had once been a staunch supporter of Indonesia's rule in East Timor.

Some in Indonesia's political elite today see a somewhat similar Australian "design" in Papua, another restive region, in easternmost Indonesia. This is despite repeated assurances from successive administrations in Canberra that Australia respects Indonesia's territorial integrity.

Trust, essential in any relationship, has been thinning

Indonesia's suspicions are not all that far-fetched when some of the dots are connected.

The Australian government's recent decision to host a US military base in Darwin, just south of Bali, fuelled speculation and conspiracy theories about Australia's colonialist intentions. No less a figure than General Gatot Nurmantyo, the chief of the Indonesian National Armed Forces, warned that the Darwin base, which houses about 1600 US marines, was too close for comfort to Papua – home to the world's largest gold reserves, operated by giant American mining company Freeport-McMoRan.

It did not help that some of the criticism of Indonesia's policy in Papua came from Australian non-governmental organisations and churches, and from Papuan rebel leaders who staged a separatist campaign from locations in Australia. This reminded Indonesians that East Timorese in exile also used Australia as the base for their campaign for independence. East Timor's Nobel Peace Prize winner, José Ramos-Horta, for instance, had a home in Australia, and his Fretilin group broadcast its messages from a radio station in Darwin. The Australian government insisted that there was a vast difference between its position on Papua and that of private organisations exercising free speech. While Jakarta officially accepted these assurances from Canberra, politicians and some military officers will from time to time accuse Australia of harbouring a hidden agenda.

Bonded by disaster: the tsunami and the Bali bombings

These periodic downturns in relations between Indonesia and Australia are, as we have seen, often played up by the media and political leaders, and often negate or neglect many of the positive developments that occur between the two countries. Some of these developments make headlines when they take place, but are quickly forgotten, or are eclipsed by the bad news.

When a destructive tsunami struck Aceh in 2004, Australia was among the first to offer aid, sending relief supplies, medical teams and heavy equipment to assist Indonesia in dealing with the devastation. This was due not only to Australia's geographical proximity but also because the two nations' militaries have built a good understanding over the years, despite events in East Timor. The mass destruction in northern Aceh meant only those with ready personnel and heavy equipment could access the quake- and tsunami-stricken areas; this was a job for the military. Defying protests by diehard nationalist politicians in Jakarta, the Indonesian National Armed Forces invited foreign military personnel to fly directly to Aceh. Australians were among the first to arrive.

The terrorist attack in Bali in October 2002 that killed more than 200 people, including scores of Australians, brought the two nations together like never before. Indonesia has always been particularly wary about letting foreign soldiers set foot on its soil, regarding this as other nations trampling on its sovereignty. But that night, the Australian Royal Air Force received the green light to fly planes into Denpasar and evacuate many of the injured to Darwin for immediate medical assistance.

The cooperation did not end there. In the wake of the Bali attack, Indonesian police received extensive assistance from foreign governments, including Australia's, to strengthen their capacity in fighting terrorists, such as by improving their intelligence capability. Today, the metal detectors in shopping malls and office buildings in large Indonesian cities indicate that terrorism remains a serious threat, but the police are widely credited for busting terrorist networks, killing the masterminds and perpetrators of the Bali bombings, and arresting hundreds of other suspects with alleged terrorist involvement. However, the suicide bombings of three churches in the East Java city of Surabaya in May 2018, killing fourteen people, including the six bombers, were a reminder that Indonesia's counterterrorist forces still have their work cut out for them.

Also not widely reported, if at all, is that Australia remains one of the largest aid donors to Indonesia, including providing assistance in building democratic institutions. Eastern Indonesians understand and appreciate Australia's economic assistance, as Canberra has focused its aid programs in the largely underdeveloped regions to the east, which are geographically closer. Yet the impact this aid has had on people's lives in these regions has largely escaped the attention of the media and the political elite back in Jakarta. (Perhaps it has also escaped attention in Australia, which cut aid to Indonesia by more than 10 per cent – from $357 million to $316 million – in the May 2018 budget.)

One of Australia's most important contributions to Indonesia goes all the way back to the early days of Indonesia's independence, in 1945. At the end of World War II Australian labour unions ordered their members working in ports to prevent the loading and shipment of arms intended for the Dutch colonial government, which was trying to reimpose its rule in Indonesia. In August 1945, the Australian Council of Trade Unions condemned the "war of aggression" against the Indonesian people. Two months later, the Indonesian president Sukarno, fresh from declaring Indonesia's independence, cabled the unions from Yogyakarta to thank them for their "magnificent, freedom-loving attitude", saying it had demonstrated that "the world's social conscience is recognising the justice of our cause". The black-ban by Australian unions was a major psychological boost for Indonesia, which was struggling to win support both on the ground and in the international arena. Yet with the passing of time, this important episode in the relationship between the two countries appears to have been largely forgotten.

Coming to Australia: Indonesians abroad

There is some evidence that the regard for Australia among Indonesia's elite is far warmer than news headlines suggest or the media cares to show. Indonesians with money to spare – and their numbers are growing – have long seen Australia as a convenient and safe place to buy property (and it has certainly been a profitable investment). At the height of the Indonesian financial crisis in the late 1990s, when the rupiah rapidly lost its value, Australian property developers took out full-page ads in

The old view of Australia as a white man's colony remains dominant

The Jakarta Post and other Indonesian newspapers to convince locals that Australia was a safe bet for any extra money they had. Property ownership in Australia also makes it easier to secure residency or even citizenship status.

Partly as a result of this, thousands of Indonesians looking for a better life have relocated to Australia with their families. It is not uncommon today, unlike twenty or thirty years ago, to hear the Indonesian language spoken in downtown Perth, Sydney or Melbourne. Many of these Indonesians have migrated permanently and taken up Australian citizenship. Australia is their first choice because of its geographical proximity, and as one of the few countries with an open immigration policy.

Australia is also the first choice as a study location for many Indonesians. Some parents send their children to schools in Australia from an early age, but most Indonesian students are undergraduates studying at some of Australia's top universities in Sydney, Melbourne, Canberra and Brisbane. The Australian government also offers generous scholarships for Indonesians to do their master's degrees in the country. Education is a large and profitable business in Australia, with international programs aimed primarily at Asian students.

In addition, with the growing ranks of the Indonesian middle class, overseas vacations have become the norm for many Indonesians. Initially, nouveau riche Indonesians would go to Singapore, Malaysia and Saudi Arabia, but their habits are changing, and Australia now ranks equal with Japan, South Korea and Europe as a holiday destination.

The final piece of good news is that relations have been improving recently thanks to the personal ties between Widodo and Prime Minister Malcolm Turnbull. The two have apparently hit it off ever since their first meeting in 2015, shortly after Turnbull's election. Under their leadership, there have been no major disputes – or at least, those that have occurred have not been significant enough for the media to exploit. In January 2017, for example, General Gatot Nurmantyo halted all military ties with Australia after an Indonesian officer training at a base in Australia informed him that the Australians were using educational material offensive to Indonesia – including a homework assignment that stated Papua should be granted independence because it was part of Melanesia. Widodo, however, weighed in, ensuring that only the joint training program with Australia was suspended.

Undoing old perceptions: trade, diplomacy and statecraft

Much to the frustration of diplomats in Jakarta and Canberra, all these positive trends have yet to change the way the Indonesian public looks at Australia. The old view of Australia as a white man's colony in Asia still remains dominant, and Indonesian political leaders often play this up, exploiting the public's ignorance whenever the two countries become entangled in another dispute.

The Indonesian elite, along with members of the media, who should know better, have been complicit, keeping silent when they could, and should, have spoken up. They bow to patriotism and cheer the government, whether they believe it is right or wrong. This is particularly true whenever their government is in dispute with Australia. Surely some in the Indonesian media could have explained the concerns Australians had about the way Indonesia slaughtered cows? Surely some would have watched the Australian documentary about the two Bali Nine members, showing how they had reformed, and could have presented this as a reason to spare their lives? Yet the media have their own motive: selling news, which means reporting the bad and ignoring the good. It is probably due to this that, for all these years, the Australia–Indonesia Institute continues to sponsor those editor meetings to try to inject some much-needed balance into the coverage of each country's affairs.

The disputes Indonesia has had with Australia reflect the intensity of the relations between these two giant neighbours. Given their geographical proximity, they are bound to have their ups and downs. If the absence of tensions is used as an indicator of how close two countries are, Indonesia has stronger relations with Iceland. For better or worse, Indonesia and Australia are condemned to be neighbours. They should make the most of their position and work on their relationship. Indonesia has also had its share of disputes with Malaysia, Singapore and now China. A better level of understanding and more knowledge about each other would certainly help both Australia and Indonesia.

For its part, Indonesians could learn to better appreciate the contribution Australia has made to their wellbeing and even prosperity, dating back to the early days of their country's independence in 1945, and continuing with the economic assistance Australia has provided for development and, since 1998, for building Indonesia into a more democratic nation. Unfortunately, most development aid programs, unlike trade and investment, have low visibility. Until Indonesia trades more with Australia, and until Indonesia sees more Australian investment, the Indonesian view of Australia as barely relevant will likely remain.

Indonesia has yet to reciprocate Australia's mantra, uttered by Paul Keating in the late 1990s and repeated by successive prime ministers, that "no country is more important to Australia than Indonesia". Irrespective of whether this is true or not, a similar statement by an

Indonesian leader about Australia could have made a vast difference to the Indonesian public perception.

Admittedly, Indonesia would never give Australia's importance such centrality. Indonesian diplomats prefer to see ASEAN as the cornerstone of its foreign policy. Next in priority are the other nine members of that association, followed by Japan, China and South Korea, and then the United States and Saudi Arabia. Australia would rank alongside European countries in terms of importance to Indonesia. But it should be noted that this is a very Jakarta-centric view. For Indonesians living in the east, perhaps from Bali and beyond, Australia is probably the most important foreign relationship. So Jakarta should at least

For better or worse, Indonesia and Australia are condemned to be neighbours

consider Australia as *one of* its most important relationships. Until such a view is articulated, most Indonesians will remain indifferent towards Australia, which helps to explain why the old perception of Australia has hardly changed across the years.

But Australia will not be an important strategic partner, compared with other countries in the region, as long as trade and economic ties between the nations remain so limited. According to Indonesia's Ministry of Trade, total trade between the two countries has actually shrunk by more than 4 per cent in the past five years. This is something both governments have been working to change, with the imminent completion of negotiations over a comprehensive economic partnership agreement.

Some Indonesian diplomats would say that Australia has always been strategically important to Indonesia's foreign policy, and indeed the two countries have joined hands in setting up organisations such as the Asia-Pacific Economic Cooperation (APEC) and the East Asia Summit. They have also collaborated in countering terrorism, in trying to contain the flow of asylum seekers from the Middle East and South Asia, and in disaster relief operations. The rise of China, and its implications for Indonesian national security, has led Indonesia, too, to review its defence cooperation with other countries, including Australia. Like other countries in Asia, Indonesia is hedging its strategic security, but it has rejected Australia's entreaty to join in an alliance with the United States, Japan and India to contain China.

But as long as the economic ties are weak, Australia cannot be all that close to Indonesia as a strategic partner. Canberra and Jakarta have been dragging their feet in concluding negotiations for the comprehensive economic partnership agreement. If and when they sign it – as they are expected to, later in 2018 – perhaps the two countries will invest in and trade with each other. Only then might relations move to the next level.

Closing the gap: how to defeat the indifference

Eventually, Indonesians' perceptions of Australia, and Australians' perceptions of Indonesia, are likely to change, even without any conscious effort by the Indonesian media or the political elite, because the differences that have divided them in the past are slowly disappearing or narrowing. Australia is becoming more diverse through immigration, and its population includes many new residents from Indonesia. The superiority and inferiority complexes that governed relations in the past will surely become a thing of the past.

Also disappearing is the unequal divide between a wealthy country and a poor country, and between aid donor and aid recipient, now that Indonesia's economic prosperity has increased and continues to rise. Its leaders now sit with Australia's in the G20, the economic council of wealthy nations. The gap will narrow further, with Indonesia expected to

As long as the economic ties are weak, Australia cannot be all that close to Indonesia as a strategic partner

rise from its current position as the sixteenth-largest economy in the world to within the top ten economies by 2025, and even the top five by 2040, based on current projections.

Last but not least, there is a convergence in values and principles, with Indonesia now a fully-fledged democracy, while Australia is an increasingly multi-racial democracy. Indonesians tend not to hold grudges against Australian politicians who have used Indonesia as a punching bag to win elections. For instance, in recent Australian elections, politicians, wanting to blame somebody, have accused Indonesia of not doing its part to stem the flow of "boat people". Indonesian leaders knew that as soon as the election was over, the newly appointed prime minister would seek to make amends by ensuring Indonesia was their first overseas visit, demonstrating the mantra that no country is more important to Australia than Indonesia.

Indonesia plays exactly the same game, with politicians picking on foreign countries or corporations for some of the problems the nation faces. Fortunately or not, since Australia is not all that important to Indonesia, politicians don't pick on Australia as much as they do on China and the United States. President Widodo's decision to declare a war on drugs and order the execution of foreign drug traffickers in 2015 was not aimed at singling out Australia, but it was a populist policy that played well with a domestic audience. Abbott took the bait, and his response only shored up Widodo's popular support.

Perceptions change slowly on both sides in Australia and Indonesia. In the absence of direct contact or strong trade, ignorance can be hard to combat. The disputes that divide the countries don't help. Indonesian political leaders exploit the public ignorance for their own interests, often at the cost of undermining positive relations. One could only wish that the middle-class elite, including the opinion-makers in the media, could help to bring the perception closer to the reality. Perhaps then Indonesia and Australia might live like two neighbours should. ■

RETREAT FROM DEMOCRACY?

The rise of Islam and the
challenge for Indonesia

Tim Lindsey

For much of the past twenty years, Indonesia has been held up as
a model of democratic transition for other countries, particularly
those with significant Muslim populations. Indonesia's leaders like
to present their nation as embodying an exemplary path away from
authoritarianism. Their form of government, they say, is tolerant yet enshrines religious practice, offering a political alternative
for Muslim communities that is more palatable to the West than
the failed Arab Spring and the extremist catastrophes that have
engulfed the Middle East since America intervened in Afghanistan
and Iraq.

This view of Indonesia now needs rethinking. The country's
hard-won advances towards liberalism and tolerance may be under
threat. This nation of more than 260 million people – more than

85 per cent of them Muslim – has often been called the "smiling face of Islam", but that label may no longer apply.

Indonesia's recent questioning of its own liberal-democratic aspirations has been accompanied by growing expressions of intolerance, including violence towards vulnerable minorities. As 2019's presidential election approaches, the temptation to resort to regressive identity politics and opportunistic populism will increase, and Indonesia's departure from its post-1998 progressive tilt is likely to become more pronounced.

To explore this shift, and the extent to which Indonesia's national identity is in contest, it is worth considering an ill-fated poetry reading in Jakarta on 30 March 2018. It took place at Indonesia Fashion Week, an event that ordinarily would have attracted little controversy – but then again, Sukmawati Sukarnoputri is no ordinary poet.

Sukma, as she is known, is the youngest daughter of Sukarno, the charismatic first president of Indonesia, a man of many contradictions and a chequered record. Exercising power from 1945 to 1966, he led Indonesia out of colonialism, through the Japanese occupation and into democracy. He then delivered it into demagoguery, initiating four decades of authoritarianism, from 1957 until 1998 (which only ended when the country's second president, Suharto, was forced to resign). At each stage, Sukarno opposed calls for an Islamic state and resisted the imposition of sharia law. Due to this, he stands today – for all his flaws – as a powerful symbol of religious pluralism and tolerance for many Indonesians, including for his children, who see themselves as inheritors of their father's legacy.

His oldest daughter, Megawati Sukarnoputri, a canny survivor and tough political player, was Indonesia's fifth president. She has always been wary of the Islamist conservatives who were her father's foes, and who at one point nearly managed to assassinate him. Sukma shares her sister's views on Islamists, and her personal dedication to the memory of her "Papi" has never been in doubt. Her small career as a dancer and a poet has undoubtedly been assisted by her surname, as have been her attempts since the late 1990s to build a political party around her father's ideas.

At the March 2018 event at the Jakarta Convention Centre, Sukma read out a poem she had published in 2006 and had recited publicly as recently as 2015. Her poem reflected the anxiety common to many members of Indonesian civil society about what they see as the threat to Indonesia posed by growing Islamic piety and intolerance. Part of it went like this:

I do not know Islamic shari'a.

What I do know is the *sari konde* [a traditional Javanese women's hairdo] of Mother Indonesia, which is beautiful.

More beautiful than your *niqab* . . .

I do not know Islamic shari'a.

What I do know is the sound of the ballad of Mother Indonesia, which is beautiful.

More beautiful than your *azan* [call to prayer].

This triggered a strong reaction from conservative Islamist groups. They alleged that Sukma, who is Muslim, had insulted Islam.

Her accusers included the notorious vigilante organisation the Islamic Defenders Front (Front Pembela Islam, FPI). It also included Islamist ginger groups such as Alumni 212 and the Anti-Defamation of Religion Forum. These latter groups were formed after their members played key roles in the 2016 and 2017 demonstrations that led to the electoral defeat of former Jakarta governor Basuki Tjahaja Purnama, known as "Ahok", and his jailing for blasphemy over his use of a verse in the Qu'ran in a speech. (The 212 Alumni group is named for the date of the largest of these protests: 2 December, in 2016.) The anger these groups felt towards Sukma was doubtless aggravated by her public support for Ahok and her criticism of FPI's leader, Rizieq Shihab, following his attacks on the ethnic Chinese Christian governor. The three organisations quickly filed eight formal complaints with the police, calling for Sukma to be prosecuted for blasphemy and hate speech.

Five days later, Sukma called a press conference and, desperate to avoid prosecution, tearfully apologised for her poem "from the bottom of my heart". The Jakarta branch of the Indonesian Ulama Council (MUI, Majelis Ulama Indonesia), Indonesia's peak organisation for *ulama* (Muslim religious scholars), accepted the apology and called for the police to drop the matter, but FPI and its supporters remained unmoved. The police investigation is officially underway, although it remains to be seen whether Sukma will ever be called into a courtroom.

Democracy and the end of innocence

A few years ago, the possibility that a daughter of Sukarno might face investigation for blasphemy would have been unimaginable to most Indonesians. But then again, the possibility that the popular governor of Jakarta, a high-profile figure on the national stage, could be doing two years behind bars for blasphemy would have seemed equally unlikely.

However, there has been a huge rise in prosecutions for blasphemy since Indonesia's second president, Suharto, and his authoritarian New Order fell twenty years ago – over a hundred, more in each decade since 1998 than for all decades before that combined. More significantly, almost all these prosecutions have resulted in convictions. This has raised real concern about the right to religious freedom, equal treatment before the law, and due process.

The post-Suharto era has been marked by a dramatic rise in religious conflict

The post-Suharto era has also been marked by a dramatic rise in religious conflict, leading to violent attacks on social and religious minorities, including Christians, unorthodox Muslims and so-called "deviant sects". Scholars have described this as "the conservative turn" in Indonesian Islam, or "the end of innocence".

How did this happen in a country often seen as a paragon of tolerance in the Muslim world? How did it happen in a nation that, in 2002, saw an overwhelming majority of its political parties vote against amending the constitution to make sharia law obligatory for Muslims?

The answer lies, perhaps ironically, in the fact that Indonesia is now democratic.

Reformasi and the price of freedom

After President Suharto's resignation in 1998, Indonesia, the globe's most populous Muslim nation, underwent a remarkable transition from military-backed authoritarianism: it became the third-largest democracy in the world, after India and the United States.

The dramatic reinvention of this complex, sprawling country was driven to a significant extent by civil society, with reformers from grassroots and non-government organisations seeing themselves as a bulwark against authoritarianism and majoritarianism. They were a disparate group, and included the leaders of mainstream "moderate" Muslim organisations such as Nahdlatul Ulama and Muhammadiyah, who between them claim around 70 million followers. Also included were much smaller "secular" NGOs, such as the Legal Aid Institute (Lembaga Bantuan Hukum, LBH), which had led dissent against the New Order and kept a liberal-democratic vision of Indonesia alive for decades. These NGOs had engaged in courageous political activism, including running doomed defences in subversion trials, in which court hearings became opportunities to present sophisticated and damning critiques of Suharto's regime.

Over the next five years, negotiations between leaders from civil society, elite survivors of Suharto's regime, legislators, wealthy oligarchs and the armed forces slowly led to the army retreating to the barracks and the piecing together of a new democratic system with clear liberal ambitions. Key to this reformation, known as *Reformasi*, was the lifting of New Order restrictions on public debate and the expression of religious identity, along with the introduction of a plethora of civil rights guarantees, between 1999 and 2002. These included guarantees of religious freedom and freedom from discrimination, and a right to due process and equality before the law, among a wide array of rights lifted almost wholesale from the Universal Declaration of Human Rights. A Constitutional Court, Indonesia's first, was established to interpret them, and a Human Rights Court, another first, to enforce them. Civil rights, which had been largely absent under Suharto's regime, were seen by *Reformasi* leaders as central to the new system's legitimacy.

This wave of reforms opened public discourse to voices long supressed by Suharto's stifling military bureaucratic system. Protests and demonstrations, usually quickly shut down under Suharto, soon became routine on the streets of Jakarta. The media also embraced the new climate of freedom, eagerly exploring a gamut of previously taboo subjects, including the corruption of Suharto and his cronies, the need for sweeping political and legal reform and the place of sharia law in Indonesian life.

At first, the loudest of the new voices belonged to proponents of liberal democracy, but it soon became clear that a space for debate had also been created for their conservative Islamist opponents, often referred to in Indonesia as "hardliners" (*garis keras*). These Muslim conservatives, committed to the Islamisation of Indonesia, had opposed Sukarno's leftist regime, with its commitment to religious pluralism, and then Suharto's right-wing New Order regime, which saw them as a threat to its tight grip on state and society. Forced underground, the hardliners emerged after 1998 with their views tainted by decades of marginalisation and repression, and little experience of pluralism and tolerance.

They quickly identified liberal democracy as the new enemy, a view epitomised by a notorious MUI fatwa in 2005 damning secularism (ise), pluralism (pi) and liberalism (lis) as un-Islamic social diseases, labelling them with the acronym "SEPILIS" (syphilis). "Teachings influenced by pluralism, liberalism and secularism are against Islam," MUI declared, adding that Muslims must consider all other faiths to be wrong. MUI is not a formal state institution, and the fatwas it issues are not legally binding, but they can be very influential in sectors of the Muslim community.

Hardliner groups, despite their small numbers, exploited the new freedoms with much savvy, skilfully using mass mobilisation, popular culture, social media and disruptive "fake news" campaigns to leverage political power. They have now captured a good deal of public space previously occupied by other civil-society groups, some Muslim, that supported liberal democracy. It is a grim paradox that the voices of openness and tolerance which sought to present

Indonesia as a paragon of Muslim democracy now find themselves facing opposition from champions of Muslim intolerance empowered by that same democracy.

Sliding towards a Neo New Order?

In Indonesia today, reform has stagnated. Although in 1998 the democratic transition was presented as a national consensus, this was never entirely true. It always had opponents, some of whom felt politically constrained to accept democratisation as a necessary evil but never saw it as a final settlement. As well as the hardliners, today these include enormously wealthy oligarchs, tenacious survivors of Suharto's regime, and elements of the armed forces.

Liberal democracy is under threat from populism, Islamism and renewed conservatism

These disparate forces that together form Indonesia's revisionist and populist right have little in common and often compete with one another. However, they also create expedient alliances, motivated by a common desire to roll back at least some of the democratic system initiated by *Reformasi*. Together they can sometimes intimidate or outflank progressive civil-society leaders. Governments, local and national, seem uncertain about how to respond to these challenges, and vacillate between inaction, opaqueness or endorsement of reactionary policies. As a result, twenty years on from *Reformasi*, the spirit of reform that drove democratisation seems distant, and a poem published without controversy in 2006 can now cause outrage.

Most Indonesian champions of civil society would agree that *Reformasi* ended long ago – maybe well over a decade ago – but a new label to define what replaced it has not yet emerged. This reflects an uncertainty among many Indonesians about where their country is heading. Many prominent critics of the government believe that while electoral democracy seems entrenched, liberal democracy is under threat from populism, Islamism and renewed conservatism. For them, Indonesia seems to be sliding towards what some call the "Neo New Order". Others say this is too harsh, arguing that electoral democracy is now firmly entrenched and the critical change that marked the end of Suharto's system, the retreat of the military from government, has not been reversed.

However, it is increasingly difficult to argue that all is well with Indonesian democracy. The forthcoming elections aside, rampant corruption is perhaps Indonesia's single biggest political issue. The courageous Corruption Eradication Commission is under continual attack from politicians and police. The human rights courts are virtually defunct and rarely hear cases. The National Commission on Human Rights is ineffective; the Constitutional Court has faced its own corruption scandals; the press is confronting increasingly prohibitive defamation laws that assist politicians and oligarchs; and civil society is under pressure from elite pushback and Islamist provocation. Small wonder, then, that Sukma rushed to make her public apology.

Islamising the state

"Neo New Order" may not be the right label, but it is clear enough that *Reformasi* is history. What is less clear is where Indonesia will eventually settle. Will liberal democracy bounce back? Will Indonesia's resilient oligarchs finally complete their creeping takeover of government? Will Indonesia follow the path of Malaysia under United Malays National Organisation rule (which ended in May, after sixty-one years), conceding significant political privilege to conservative Islam and gradually institutionalising intolerance though discriminatory laws, policies and practices? Or will the country just keep muddling through?

As things stand, it is unlikely that Indonesia will formally become an Islamic state anytime soon, or even grant Islam or sharia law the constitutional privilege that Sukarno always opposed. Militant fringe organisations, such as Jemaah Islamiyah – which carried out the 2000 church bombings, the 2002 Bali bombings and the 2004 Australian Embassy bombing in Jakarta – and Jemaah Anshurat Daulah – one of the groups that embarked on a campaign of Islamic State–inspired suicide bombings of Christians and police in May this year – are among a long line of rebel groups committed to building an Islamic state in Indonesia. But for all the publicity they attract, and the damage they do to Indonesia's international image, these terrorists have very limited impact on the lives of ordinary Indonesian Muslims, and no real prospect of achieving their main objective. There is little public support for an Islamic state. The word "Islam" does not even appear in Indonesia's constitution, and there is no appetite to re-open the difficult constitutional amendment process that convulsed Indonesian politics for the four years after Suharto's resignation, leading to the rejection of a proposal to make sharia law mandatory for Muslims.

The preamble to the constitution does, however, impose an obligation on Indonesians to believe in an "Almighty God". This is the first limb of the *Pancasila*, the national ideology and foundational philosophical theory of the Indonesian state. It means that atheism is a criminal offence, and that the six official religions, particularly Islam, enjoy formal legal and governmental support. (The other religions are Protestantism, Catholicism, Hinduism, Buddhism and, strangely, Confucianism, which in most other countries is a philosophy, not a faith.) Likewise, the Constitutional Court has held that Indonesia is neither an Islamic state nor a secular one, but has declared it a "religious country".

This valorisation of religion offers obvious opportunities for conservative Islamists. Instead of the Islamic state that militants demand, they have opted for a more nuanced strategy of Islamising the state. They use political activism (including demonstrations, social media campaigns and lobbying), accusations of blasphemy, and legal reform to gradually impose laws and norms based on conservative Islamic values. These include restrictions on clothing and public expressions of sexuality, and the banning of alcohol, among others. As a model for this approach many look to Malaysia, particularly the conservative

northern states of Terengganu and Kelantan, which sought to intro-
duce harsh sharia criminal codes in the 1990s. This approach has been
most effective at the local level in Indonesia, where Islamising local
laws (so-called *perda syariah*) is the preferred tool of the *syariahisasi*
(shariaisation) movement.

Such strategies have encouraged religious intolerance and led
to social tensions, community violence and criminal prosecutions
of minorities. In some regions, it has even led to armed civil conflict
based on ethnic or religious dif-
ference, with the state usually
declining to intervene or tacitly
(in some cases, overtly) supporting Islamist intolerance – for
example, in relation to attacks on

**Indonesia is neither
an Islamic state
nor a secular one**

Shi'as and Ahmadis, minority groups whose identification as Muslim
is rejected by most Indonesian Sunnis.

In one notorious case in 2008, a hardliner vigilante group that
included many members of FPI attacked a peaceful multi-faith rally in
the centre of Jakarta. The families marching were calling for religious
tolerance, particularly towards Ahmadis, but attackers used sticks, broken glass and swords to seriously injure thirty-four men, women and
children, citing MUI fatwas against Ahmadi beliefs as justification.
Over a thousand police were present but did little to stop the violence.

The hardliners are also assisted by the Constitutional Court's ruling in 2010 that Indonesia's controversial blasphemy laws are valid.

This handed hardliners a powerful weapon to use against those they see as enemies – Sukma, for example.

The recent jailing of Ahok demonstrates the problem. During the Jakarta gubernatorial election campaign, footage of Ahok commenting on the interpretation of a Qur'anic verse was posted online by one of his critics. In it, Ahok, who is Christian, refuted claims by his opponents that the verse barred Muslims from voting for a non-Muslim. However, the footage was carefully edited to suggest he said that people could be "fooled" by the Qur'an. The video went viral. Hardliner groups claimed Ahok had insulted the Qur'an and, backed by powerful politicians linked to the rival candidates, led huge rallies in the nation's capital. Ahok, vulnerable for his Chinese ethnicity as well as his religion, became an easy target, and the 2 December 2016 demonstration drew around 700,000 protesters onto the streets.

The government of President Joko Widodo ("Jokowi") struggled to respond effectively, apparently intimidated by the attacks on Ahok, once Jokowi's close colleague, and by calls for the toppling of Jokowi himself. Abandoned by the president, Ahok lost the election and became the first Indonesian politician to be jailed for a religious offence.

Many Indonesians saw Ahok's fall as emblematic of the increase in religious and social intolerance in post-Suharto Indonesia. This, they believe, now threatens the pluralist bargain that underpinned the formation of the Indonesian polity. Pew Research Center surveys suggest that Indonesians, compared with Muslims worldwide, have become far less tolerant of other religions. They are, for example, significantly less accepting of interfaith marriage or living in proximity to members of other faiths than Pakistani Muslims, according to Pew. The same is true for their attitudes to unorthodox Muslim sects. A survey this year by State Islamic University Jakarta found that 33 per cent of young Muslims believed that acts of intolerance against minorities were "not a problem", and 34 per cent felt that apostates should be killed. These findings have profound implications for Indonesian politics and, indeed, for the ideas that are at the heart of the republic itself.

Are the many still one?

At the time of Indonesia's birth, Sukarno and the other founders of Indonesia were deeply concerned by the problem of how to knit a fractious, disparate archipelago of extraordinary ethnic, religious and social diversity into a single nation that would inherit the footprint of the Netherlands East Indies.

From the early 1600s onwards, the Dutch had gradually conquered hundreds of societies across the vast chain of islands that comprises the Indonesian archipelago. Some of these societies had much in common, but many had developed quite independently for centuries before the Dutch forced them into a single colonial state. The nationalist leaders who had struggled against the repressive colonial government since the 1920s were aware of these differences. They knew that fragmentation was a more natural postcolonial course than unity.

As the war in the Pacific ended in 1945, these leaders were encouraged by the occupying Japanese to declare independence. In the tumultuous months leading up to the declaration of independence on 17 August that year, they argued about how to hold their putative new state together. Their disagreements were many, but mutual difference – a product of the profound social diversity of the archipelago – was emphasised as the common national quality that would unite their country. This ideology was embodied by the state motto *"Bhinneka Tunggal Eka"* ("out of many, one", or "unity in diversity"), a phrase lifted from a fourteenth-century Javanese poem, or *kakawin*, that called for religious tolerance.

Bhinneka Tunggal Eka was a principle Sukarno relied on to rule, first as a democrat and then as a demagogue. Suharto later distorted it further to legitimise the banning of public discussion of ethnicity, race or religion, and the systematic repression of political Islam. It nonetheless remains an evocative political idea, and one most Indonesians have had drummed into them since childhood. However, the question often being asked now is: who should be counted among the many? Who can be accepted as true Indonesians? For hardliners, the answer is simple: orthodox, conservative indigenous Sunni Muslims.

In recent years, the hardliners have been emboldened by the government's timidity on religious issues and the cowing of civil society by resurgent political elites, who are beginning to deploy legal measures against their critics, including defamation laws and a new power to ban NGOs without judicial process. This emboldening has led hardliners to ratchet up the targeting of vulnerable outsiders, such as unorthodox Muslim groups and minority religions, especially Christianity. Certain minorities have attracted particular opprobrium from newly confident conservatives, including ethnic Chinese, like Ahok, and lesbian, gay, bisexual and trans and/or intersex (LGBTI) groups. For example, a conservative Muslim organisation, the Family Love Alliance, recently submitted a petition to the Constitutional Court seeking to make same-sex relationships illegal. They failed, but the national legislature is now considering amendments to the broadcasting law that would ban all LGBTI content. The legislators have also conducted an acrimonious debate over plans to criminalise homosexuality.

Who can be accepted as true Indonesians? For hardliners, the answer is simple

Proposed criminal code amendments seem to have been watered down, but the latest draft, if passed, could still be used to prosecute any public display of homosexuality.

These developments could have major implications for the lives of LGBTI Indonesians. They would mark a radical shift in Indonesian attitudes, which have historically been relatively tolerant of LGBTI communities, particularly *waria*, or transgender women, some of whom achieved media celebrity in the past.

Yet perhaps the most chilling development has been the targeting of gay men and transgender women in Aceh. Sharia law occupies a unique place in this province. The long-running secessionist conflict between the Free Aceh Movement and Jakarta was finally resolved after the 2004 tsunami devastated the area and forced the two sides to the negotiating table in Helsinki. The settlement deal confirmed that Aceh would stay part of the republic in return for a high degree of autonomy and the right to apply its own version of sharia law. Other provinces can pass local laws that reflect Islamic norms to a limited degree, but only Aceh can apply sharia as a valid source of law in its own right.

Sharia courts and a religious police force were established in Aceh, and local regulations called *qanun* were passed. These impose criminal punishments that include public caning for a range of moral and religious transgressions; unlike in the rest of Indonesia, the religious offences include certain kinds of homosexual sex. In 2017, images of two terrified gay men being caned on a platform in front of a hooting, mocking crowd brandishing smartphones made front-page news around the world. Jakarta declined to intervene.

Although homosexuality is not yet a criminal offence outside Aceh, the rising climate of conservative intolerance means the LGBTI community elsewhere is targeted in other ways. In Jakarta, for example, under the pornography law raids on saunas and clubs have led to near-naked gay men being arrested for immoral behaviour and paraded before the media. This law bans not only pornography (which was already illegal, in any case) but also any form of public eroticism, popularly known as *pornoaksi*, or "pornographic action", giving police sweeping powers to target sexual minorities and other vulnerable groups.

The controversial pornography law, passed in 2008, was opposed at the time by civil society groups, particularly women's NGOs and the legal aid network, but was equally strongly supported by the Islamist right. This was arguably the hardliners' first major national victory, an important step in their emergence as a rising political force.

Indonesia's alt-right – trolls, hackers and vigilantes

The tensions over Islam are part of a much older struggle in Indonesia to determine who controls the interpretation of the religion, and thus religious power. However, the recent rise of conservative Islamist hardliners also resembles the rise of populism and conservative politics elsewhere in the world. Islamist conservatives are in many ways the local equivalent of America's alt-right – and they are just as adept at online disruption and manipulation.

Research by State Islamic University Jakarta links the rise of religious intolerance among young Muslims to their increased access to the internet and social media. Indeed, Jakarta tweets more than any other city in the world, and Indonesians are very big users of Facebook, as well as WhatsApp, Instagram and Telegram, an encrypted-messaging service.

One of the best-known examples of online disruption involves the so-called Muslim Cyber Army, the most prominent of a number of tags adopted by Islamist trolls in Indonesia. Active across all platforms popular in Indonesia, Muslim Cyber Army members enjoy building an atmosphere of mystery, threat and self-importance, sometimes using the Guy Fawkes mask, popularised by the graphic novel and film *V for Vendetta*, of the hacktivist group Anonymous in their postings. This is deeply ironic, given the distance between their ideological objectives and the libertarian ambitions of most Western hacktivist groups. The Muslim Cyber Army does, however, share a willingness to exploit online anonymity to enable criminal activity – for example, by hijacking the social media accounts of the dead.

An Indonesian researcher, Damar Juniarto, has shown that Muslim Cyber Army trolls are highly effective, working collectively and using tools such as Twitbots to flood Twitter with coordinated messages. They target their more liberal opponents by "doxing": publishing their personal information and contact details. This often triggers physical attacks from groups such as FPI within a few days and, in some cases, police arrests on suspicion of blasphemy. A list of such targets went viral in a video produced by the "Blasphemer Hunter Team". These groups have attacked Ahok, Jokowi, foreigners and LGBTI Indonesians, targets they share with some prominent hard-liner "buzzers", or social media opinion leaders, many of whom are keyboards for hire.

Juniarto also suggests that many of these groups have close ties to politicians and senior military figures. Certainly, social media manipulation and "fake news" hoaxes produced by Islamist groups were powerful factors in the campaign that led to Ahok's defeat in last year's Jakarta gubernatorial elections. He was defeated by Anies

Baswedan, a protégé of former general Prabowo Subianto, Jokowi's rival in the 2014 presidential election.

It would be naive to think this won't happen again in the upcoming 2018 local elections and in next April's crucial legislative and presidential races. During the 2014 presidential campaign, Jokowi, a Muslim, endured claims he was a closet Christian and ethnic Chinese (his detractors chose to ignore the fact that his opponent, also a Muslim, has a Christian mother and siblings). The upcoming presidential election – which may well be a rematch between Jokowi and Prabowo, but for the first time held simultaneously with legislative elections – is expected to see the most vicious cyber campaigning yet.

> Religious conservatism, a reactionary elite and a "chilling" of civil society now threaten legal protection for minorities

Bracing for the new Indonesia

The success of the hardliners, and their skill in manipulating online opinion, has caught the much larger and more moderate Muslim movements flat-footed. Their belated efforts to stem the attacks on Ahok failed, and their leaders now fear too much influence has been ceded to MUI and the vigilante groups that work with it. While Nahdlatul Ulama and Muhammadiyah leaders refused to support the anti-Ahok rallies publicly, many of their members proudly took part.

Under Suharto, MUI, the peak organisation for Muslim scholars, was little more than a regime puppet, but after his fall it reinvented itself as the voice of the "conservative turn". Its current influence is evident in the role it plays in most blasphemy prosecutions. There is a clear pattern. First, an MUI branch issues a fatwa that sparks attacks or protests. This triggers police intervention and the arrest of the alleged blasphemer. Inevitably, the courts follow the fatwa's findings and convict, even though fatwas have no legal force in Indonesia. It was an MUI fatwa that sealed Ahok's fate, and Sukma has likely only escaped because one has not been issued against her.

Much of this can be traced back to President Yudhoyono's reluctance to move against hardline Islamist vigilante groups and his endorsement of MUI as a "guide to state policy" as a way of winning approval from conservative Muslims. In 2005, he said: "We want to place MUI in a central role in matters of Islamic faith". He went further in 2007, stating that "after a fatwa is issued, the tools of state can do their duty ... We must all take strict measures against deviant beliefs." Yudhoyono has always been at pains to present himself as a committed democrat and a supporter of human rights. This is true in some ways, but it was under his administration (2004 to 2014) that the hardliners really got the traction denied them by Yudhoyono's predecessors, Abdurrahman Wahid and Megawati Sukarnoputri.

In 2008, academics Andrew MacIntyre and Douglas Ramage wrote a perceptive paper titled "Seeing Indonesia as a Normal Country". In it, they argued that *Reformasi* Indonesia had committed to a liberal-democratic path and to participation in the international community. Pluralism and tolerance were "the bedrock fact of Indonesian society", and Australia needed to rethink dated Suharto-era attitudes to Indonesia.

Ten years later, another rethink is necessary. We need to review the persistent tropes of Indonesia as completing a successful transition to a liberal version of democracy. Rising religious conservatism, a reactionary elite and a "chilling" of civil society now threaten the achievements of *Reformasi* and, in particular, legal protection for minorities. Indonesia is certainly not turning into an Iran-style Islamic theocracy, but it might be sliding slowly towards a Malaysia-style illiberal democracy that privileges Islam and denies rights to vulnerable minorities.

Australia should once again recalibrate its expectations of its largest neighbour as Indonesia contemplates a very uncertain post-*Reformasi* future that may well prove to be more religious, less liberal and a good deal less enthusiastic about engagement with foreign nations, including us. We need to be aware that, ironically, even as Indonesia becomes a wealthier, more middle-class society, its always turbulent relations with its neighbours may prove to be more difficult in the decade ahead than at any time since the last century.

The median age of Indonesians is thirty-one. As many as 40 per cent are under twenty-four, and more than 85 per cent are Muslim. Many of them will be voting for the first time next year, and would have been just a few years old or not even born when Suharto fell.

They thus have dangerously little experience of his repressive New Order and the extraordinary events that dismantled it – their country's rejection of authoritarianism in favour of liberal-democratic aspirations. Instead, they have grown up in the post-*Reformasi* environment of clunky and increasingly illiberal procedural democracy, amid contests over Islamisation and amid the rise of the hardliners. While they are savvy and highly connected, maybe even more so than their Australian contemporaries, they are also surprisingly conservative.

Next year's elections will be a crucial moment for Indonesia: a chance for this generation to pass judgement. How young Indonesians respond to the tensions and the challenges of increasing populist intolerance, driven by Muslim conservativism, will determine the country's social and political configuration for decades ahead. Young people are the ones who will decide how to label post-*Reformasi* Indonesia, and it is by no means clear what they will decide. ∎

Reviews

Myanmar's Enemy Within:
Buddhist Violence and the
Making of a Muslim "Other"
Francis Wade
Zed Books

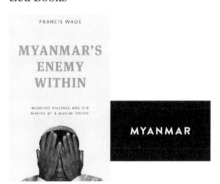

Around fifteen years ago, a petty criminal named Kaung Latt was sweating away in a filthy prison in Myanmar's Irrawaddy Delta when he was presented with an offer that was hard to refuse: early release, a house of his own, fields to till, a stipend and regular food rations in exchange for – nothing.

All he had to do in return was be himself: a Buddhist and a member of the country's Bamar ethnic majority. He was shipped hundreds of miles west, to a sea-hugging finger of tropical land known as Rakhine, where Myanmar's military regime had begun to fear it was losing control on multiple fronts.

"I was told that in Rakhine there are so many Muslims, so we want to balance that out by sending Buddhists here," Kaung Latt told journalist Francis Wade, who found him years later, still living in the "model village" of Aung Thar Yar, which had been overrun by crime, alcoholism and squalor – but was still, at least, Buddhist and Bamar.

The goal, Wade makes clear in *Myanmar's Enemy Within* – a sober account of ethnic mistrust and communal violence in Myanmar – was not only to de-Muslimise Rakhine State but to de-Rakhine it. The country's paranoid clique of ruling generals was determined to render this desperately poor outpost of empire – inhabited by a blend of Rakhine Buddhists and Rohingya Muslims who coexisted mostly peacefully, if uneasily – more tractable to its aims. Wade deploys examples such as this to trace how ethnicity and religion have become reified in Myanmar and are seen by successive governments as shorthand for state affiliation, or lack thereof.

The most obvious consequence of this sclerotic and essentialist view of ethnic identity is the ongoing Rohingya exodus, perhaps the world's worst humanitarian crisis in a generation. *Myanmar's Enemy Within* was published just before the most recent and serious outbreak of violence in August 2017, which has seen nearly 700,000 Rohingya Muslims forced out of Myanmar after being brutalised by a wave of pograms in which villages were torched by soldiers and the inhabitants raped and killed.

Wade might seem to have run up against a journalist's worst nightmare: spending years writing a book on a relatively obscure topic, only to have history overtake him and the situation explode into bloody and world-galvanising violence

after he went to print. But this is ultimately an advantage. The lack of focus on recent events means that *Myanmar's Enemy Within* does the harder work of grappling with the immensely complicated roots of the crisis. The conflict in Rakhine cannot be understood outside the context of centuries of conquest and efforts to regulate the state's indigenous population, which made this area particularly fertile for mass paranoia and anxiety about being overwhelmed demographically.

Much coverage of the Rohingya crisis has been frustratingly ahistorical. This is partly because the scale of the suffering is so vast and the victims of the atrocities so vulnerable and desperate that their misery cries out for attention. But it also means that most international readers only partially understand the history of Rakhine. Even worse, Myanmar, when it is seen at all, is often viewed through a Manichaean lens: decades of oppressive military dictatorship (bad) during which the entire population, bolstered by the moral authority of the Buddhist monkhood (good) and the leadership of the enlightened Nobel laureate Aung San Suu Kyi (good), is finally emerging into democracy (very good).

The simplicity of this narrative can lead to the impression that the convulsions of anti-Rohingya violence that began in August 2017 were an incomprehensible divergence from the Suu Kyi–led path to democracy, just as the obstacles to peace had seemed to fall away. Actually, the Rohingya crisis was not a shocking rupture so much as a collision of several long-simmering issues: tension between the centre and the periphery of an artificially drawn nation-state; growing Buddhist extremism; a perception of Buddhism as linked to citizenship and identity; and a decades-long national obsession with classifying citizens by race and religion, a ruinous vestige of British colonial rule.

To the close watcher, even the Suu Kyi of 2018 snaps into focus not as a fallen idol, but as a leader who has always been imperious and image-obsessed, dubious that Muslims had a true place in a Bamar-majority nation, deferential to certain types of military might and obsessed with preserving the legacy of her father, General Aung San, and his vision to unite Myanmar's disparate peoples into one, by force if necessary.

Many of Myanmar's tensions had been kept in check by decades of brutal military rule, which united large swathes of the population in their hatred of the junta, with Suu Kyi acting as their standard-bearer. But after 2015, Wade writes, "the military, in its retreat from power, seemed to have passed a torch onto the masses of people who had spent so many years opposing its mercurial rule".

Wade is particularly insightful on the many ways in which Burma's leaders have exploited ethnic divisions to shore up power, even as they reified the founding myth of a happily multiethnic nation. A thousand years ago, Wade notes, the man who most Burmese recognise as their first king, Anawrahta, used an emerging Buddhist identity to forcibly unite the disparate tribes of the Irrawaddy Valley into a single empire for the first time. The model villages of Rakhine are almost ur-examples of this tendency, and the story of Kaung Latt's get-out-of-jail-free card – his own ethnicity – casts into relief just how paranoid and bizarre were some of the military regime's efforts to maintain political power through what they called "Burmanisation".

Wade also shows how this program spilled over into neighbouring Chin State to target Christians there, and how "Burmanisation" involved subduing Mon groups and denying citizenship to people of Indian descent. He takes us to 1980s Yangon to meet a Mon girl miserably trying to integrate into the Bamar majority, and to 2013 Meiktila, which experienced some of the worst bouts of anti-Muslim violence outside Rakhine.

These stories convey just how vast Myanmar is – and not just physically. Rakhine, like many parts of Myanmar's periphery, feels very far from Yangon. Palm-dotted and sea-oriented, it sprawls out against the vividly blue Bay of Bengal, with a spicy, briny cuisine distinct from the oily curries of the interior, and hundreds of temples built by the ancestors of the Rakhine, who have their own dialect.

Today the Rakhine, like many of Myanmar's other ethnic groups, see themselves as descendants of a proud and ancient race. When I visited two years ago, just as the most recent crisis was rearing its head, I was struck by how beleaguered they felt: oppressed by a central government that had spent years trying to "Burmanise" them, ignored or demonised by

the international community and hemmed in by what they perceived as a terrifying influx of Muslim interlopers.

Myanmar's Enemy Within falls short in some minor respects. Wade fails to provide a convincing explanation of why anti-Muslim sentiment seems so much more brutal and contagious than other ethnic rivalries in Myanmar. (Then again, there may simply be no good explanation.) The narrative in some parts is thin and lacking in detail. This is almost certainly due to the difficulty of working in Rakhine State. During my time reporting there, a wary peace prevailed, but both Rakhine and Rohingya communities were shaken and mistrustful of outsiders, and a heavy police and military presence made travel difficult. Now that those tensions have erupted again into outright violence, access is infinitely worse, and foreign journalists are barred from entering other than during government-sponsored press tours.

In large part because of this lack of access, the story has once again become one of good versus evil: the Rohingya versus everyone else. This is not a false account, but it is not the whole truth. That is why *Myanmar's Enemy Within* is welcome: at times the

Never miss an issue. Subscribe and save.

☐ **1 year auto-renewing print and digital subscription** (3 issues) $49.99 incl. GST (save 28%)

☐ **1 year print and digital subscription** (3 issues) $59.99 incl. GST (save 13%)

☐ **2 year print and digital subscription** (6 issues) $114.99 incl. GST (save 17%)

☐ Tick here to commence subscription with the current issue.

ALL PRICES INCLUDE POSTAGE AND HANDLING.

PAYMENT DETAILS I enclose a cheque/money order made out to Schwartz Publishing Pty Ltd.
Or please debit my credit card (MasterCard, Visa or Amex accepted).

CARD NO. ☐☐☐☐ ☐☐☐☐ ☐☐☐☐ ☐☐☐☐

EXPIRY DATE   /   CCV   AMOUNT $

CARDHOLDER'S NAME

SIGNATURE

NAME

ADDRESS

EMAIL   PHONE

Freecall: 1800 077 514 **or** +61 3 9486 0288 **Email:** subscribe@australianforeignaffairs.com **australianforeignaffairs.com**
Digital-only subscriptions are available from our website: australianforeignaffairs.com/subscribe

An inspired gift. Subscribe a friend.

☐ **1 year print and digital subscription** (3 issues) $59.99 incl. GST (save 13%)

☐ **2 year print and digital subscription** (6 issues) $114.99 incl. GST (save 17%)

☐ Tick here to commence subscription with the current issue.

ALL PRICES INCLUDE POSTAGE AND HANDLING.

PAYMENT DETAILS I enclose a cheque/money order made out to Schwartz Publishing Pty Ltd.
Or please debit my credit card (MasterCard, Visa or Amex accepted).

CARD NO. ☐☐☐☐ ☐☐☐☐ ☐☐☐☐ ☐☐☐☐

EXPIRY DATE   /   CCV   AMOUNT $

CARDHOLDER'S NAME   SIGNATURE

NAME

ADDRESS

EMAIL   PHONE

RECIPIENT'S NAME

RECIPIENT'S ADDRESS

RECIPIENT'S EMAIL   PHONE

Freecall: 1800 077 514 **or** +61 3 9486 0288 **Email:** subscribe@australianforeignaffairs.com **australianforeignaffairs.com**
Digital-only subscriptions are available from our website: australianforeignaffairs.com/gift

Delivery Address:
LEVEL 1, 221 DRUMMOND ST
CARLTON VIC 3053

Australian Foreign Affairs
REPLY PAID 90094
CARLTON VIC 3053

Delivery Address:
LEVEL 1, 221 DRUMMOND ST
CARLTON VIC 3053

Australian Foreign Affairs
REPLY PAID 90094
CARLTON VIC 3053

intricacies of ethnicity in Myanmar can seem confoundingly complex, thick with the history of centuries of migrations and countless grievances; but so too is the world, and its variously constructed nations.

Julia Wallace

The People vs. Democracy: Why Our Freedom Is in Danger & How to Save It
Yascha Mounk
Harvard University Press

How Democracies Die
Steven Levitsky and Daniel Ziblatt
Crown Publishing

For some time, thinking people who feel responsibility for the fate of our planet have been asking whether democracy, as it has long been understood and valued, is stumbling towards impotence, or outright irrelevance. Opinions differ about the sources of this mounting global unease. Some observers claim to know its root causes, or treat it as a passing aberration. Others find themselves perplexed by the disorder that comes mixed with promise. As if to prove Machiavelli's observation that the road to hell is easy, since it is downhill and followed with eyes shut, still others simply do not care. Yet there is general agreement that rot and decay are spreading within states that call themselves democracies. Things are not going well.

A measure of our darkening times is the way American political scientists, once the trumpeters of good news about the global triumph of democracy, are now speaking in mournful tones about the fading of the democratic dream. Yascha Mounk writes that liberal democracy did "more to spread peace and prosperity than any other in the history of humanity". He writes in the spirit of lament for a time when the most powerful liberal democracy, the United States of America, functioned as a "shining city upon a hill" (as President Reagan said in a farewell from the Oval Office). Now, by contrast, this model is suffering an "existential crisis". The type of government that uniquely mixed "individual rights" (liberalism) and "popular rule" (democracy) and that "long characterized most governments in North America and Western Europe" is "coming apart at its seams".

What drives this disintegration? Mounk, a lecturer at Harvard University, sides with the spirit and substance of liberalism ("protecting individual rights" through the rule of law) against democracy and its populist fetish of government based on popular will. His critique warns of the dangers of democracy without rights: in a growing number of countries, including the United States, "individual rights and the rule of law are now under concerted attack from populist strongmen".

Mounk is surely right about the trends, but his diagnosis of the current malaise relies too heavily on a simple tale about the tragic estrangement of the once happily married couple liberalism and democracy. Elsewhere in the book, sensibly, he identifies the many real-world forces that are stoking discontent inside democracies: a drift towards technocracy; a deep disaffection with politicians' poor narratives and leadership skills; the hollowing out of mass-membership political parties; the collapse of cartel party systems that once served as instruments for integrating and reconciling social differences. So (we can add) are dragnet surveillance, militarised policing, rising incarceration rates, and state clampdowns on public assembly, which together make democracies feel more repressive. The long war on terrorism adds to the pressures on civil liberties, strengthening the hand of garrison states that are neither liberal nor democratic. And local institutions, such as parliaments, are being swallowed by cross-border chains of corporate and governmental power wholly unaccountable to citizens.

All these forces of disaffection have economic drivers, but Mounk's analysis has trouble making the connections. The market power of corporations goes missing in his rather nineteenth-century definition of liberalism as "basic values like freedom of speech, the separation of powers, or the protection of individual rights". He knows well that four decades of privatisation have resulted almost everywhere in predatory banks, widening gaps between rich and poor, and the emergence of a substantial "precariat" of under-employed and part-time workers in poorly paid jobs with little long-term security. Most observers associate these trends with what is widely called neoliberalism, a label that acknowledges the strong affinities that modern liberalism has with private property, markets and the ethos of possessive individualism. Yet Mounk's liberalism is too purist to acknowledge these affinities. It has a casuist quality: he seems unable to call things by their proper name. To do so would scramble his neat thesis of the unfinished historic struggle between the demons of democracy and the angels of liberalism.

Mounk is understandably preoccupied with the diabolical dynamics inside the United States, but is oblivious to the equally worrying devilish forces operating at the global level. Something else is happening that is bigger, and more harmful to democracy, as Steven Levitsky and Daniel Ziblatt emphasise in their provocatively titled *How Democracies Die*. They analyse the reasons for the breakdown of democracy in states as different as Turkey, Venezuela, Argentina and Russia. "We must learn from other countries to see the warning signs – and recognize the false alarms," they write. Their point is that the sufferings of democracy are not only an American problem. Democracy is confronted by a new world disorder that is emerging from "the collapse of the Soviet Union, the crisis of the EU, the rise of China, and the growing aggressiveness of Russia".

Levitsky and Ziblatt, both Harvard professors, have little to say about the renewed belligerence of American power during recent decades and whether its global empire is bad for democracy. Like most other Americans who no longer read Gore Vidal, they seem to think talk of empire is not cool. Levitsky and Ziblatt do ask whether we are witnessing "the decline and fall of one of the world's oldest and most successful democracies", yet they leave the question unanswered. Nevertheless, they remind us, valuably, that democracies can die slow deaths "at the hands not of generals but of elected leaders". They say many interesting things about extreme political polarisation, which has a murderous impact on democracy, and the importance of "institutional forbearance" in preventing abuses of power. And their analysis makes one thing clear: despite the haughty talk of the end of history, the once popular presumption (championed by Francis Fukuyama and other American liberal scholars and politicians) that "liberal democracy" would enjoy a global triumph has collapsed. Instead, our world is witnessing the growth of new types of anti-democratic regime – "laboratories of authoritarianism", whose surprising levels of public support and resilience in the face of serious economic, environmental and social problems suggest they are more durable than outside observers suppose.

Levitsky and Ziblatt are wrong to call these alternatives to power-sharing democracy "autocracies", "dictatorships" and "authoritarianism". China, Iran, Russia and Saudi Arabia are not the opposite of democracy. They are phantom democracies. Their crafty rulers are busily experimenting with a wide range of locally made democratic tools designed to win the trust and loyalty of their subjects. Examples include the injection of accountability mechanisms into state bureaucracy, the toleration of independent public-opinion leaders, the growing reliance on opinion polls and "democratic style" among state officials and corporate executives, and the calculated use of digitally networked media as early warning devices. These methods seem to favour rule from above. They help explain why 21st-century authoritarian regimes are globally significant political laboratories: the testing grounds for a new type of top-down popular government claiming to be superior to constitutional democracies, which once seemed so sure of themselves and are now struggling to survive in a dangerously uncertain world.

John Keane

Directorate S: The C.I.A. and America's Secret Wars in Afghanistan and Pakistan

Steve Coll

Penguin Press

Afghanistan, March 2002: Al Qaeda has been largely defeated and dispersed; the Taliban regime has fallen and its leadership wants to talk; and the international community has come in strongly behind the United States, promising aid and installing Hamid Karzai as interim head of a new Afghan government, pending a new constitution and elections. US defense secretary Donald Rumsfeld is unequivocal: "The war is over."

Afghanistan, March 2006: the Taliban has returned to the battlefield, better armed and more professional, and conflict is intense. Though NATO is nominally leading the international coalition, the United States is still in charge – but there is uncertainty in Washington about the nature and purpose of the war in Afghanistan. An election has seen Karzai formally become president, but has exposed the deep divisions in Afghan society and left his administration dependent on northerners; and in Kabul and the provinces, corruption is booming. The road ahead is looking long and hard.

So, what went wrong?

The answer matters because it explains why American and some other coalition forces – including Australia's – are still in Afghanistan today. For readers less familiar with the Afghan project, *Directorate S*, Steve Coll's successor to his Pulitzer Prize–winning *Ghost Wars*, offers a fascinating explanation. For those more closely engaged in the saga, the granular detail provided in this "journalistic history" will add colour and fill in many gaps.

Hubris was almost certainly part of what went wrong, and the absence of a plan past the successes of the first months of the American-led operation hurt. So did the preoccupation with Iraq. Coll says that by mid-2002, "the Bush administration had stopped thinking seriously about Afghanistan".

But the story Coll tells goes much deeper. He explains how American, Pakistani and Afghan intelligence agencies "influenced the rise of a new war in Afghanistan after the fall of the Taliban, and how that war fostered a revival of Al Qaeda, allied terrorist networks, and, eventually, branches of the Islamic State". Central to this is Pakistan's Inter-Services Intelligence unit, ISI, working through its secretive paramilitary wing, Directorate S.

ISI wanted a regime in Kabul that was friendly to Pakistan and embraced Pashtuns. After 2002, it became increasingly apparent that Karzai, with his Indian connections and a regime dependent on Panjshiris and the pro-India Northern Alliance, was never going to serve Pakistan's interests.

Nor could Pakistan trust the United States, either to manage Karzai or to stay the course in Afghanistan. After the invasion of Iraq, Pakistan's army chief, General Ashfaq Parvez Kayani, harboured serious doubts about America's capacity to maintain involvement in two wars concurrently – why else had NATO been called up? These doubts were compounded when the

United States cut a nuclear deal with India in 2006. And whatever goodwill might have been engendered by Washington's military and economic aid to Pakistan was overshadowed by the war in Iraq, frequent well-publicised "battlefield mistakes" in Afghanistan, cross-border military incursions against the Pakistan Taliban, and CIA excesses in Pakistan.

And so Pakistan's Directorate S moved from sheltering the Taliban leadership in Pakistan to providing more arms, training, intelligence and tactical guidance in Afghanistan. Washington tried to be tough but the coalition's logistic routes through Pakistan were critical to its presence in Afghanistan, and pressing the regime in Islamabad to the point of toppling could leave Pakistan's nuclear arsenal in even less friendly hands.

"On Al Qaeda," Coll writes, the CIA and ISI "could do business, but on the Taliban, [they] settled … into a dead embrace informed by accusation and denial." It comes as no surprise, he concludes, that "the failure to solve the riddle of ISI and to stop its covert interference in Afghanistan became, ultimately, the greatest strategic failure of the American war".

As the backdrop to this, *Directorate S* offers an illuminating account of the fractious relationships between (and within) American agencies both in Washington and on the ground in Afghanistan. Coll describes the "semi-independent campaigns waged simultaneously by different agencies of American government", and details the corrosive differences between these "stovepipes", which he says, intriguingly, were not just "tolerated" but "even promoted" by successive US administrations.

Not least of these inter-agency differences was whether to seek a "political settlement" with the Taliban. The history of this debate, from its beginnings in 2001 to the largely ill-fated negotiations that began, falteringly, in late 2010, is a fascinating subplot within Coll's larger story.

In the early years post-2001, resistance came from the White House, and from Rumsfeld and Vice President Dick Cheney, notwithstanding support for negotiations from the Saudis, Qataris and even some in the CIA. President Barack Obama's 2008 appointment of veteran American diplomat Richard Holbrooke as his Special Representative for Afghanistan and Pakistan brought new energy to the idea of a negotiated settlement. Based on his experience fifty years earlier as civilian adviser in Vietnam and with history on his side, Holbrooke believed that insurgencies could not be beaten by military means alone. But Obama and Secretary of State Hillary Clinton hesitated about taking on a sceptical Congress and the Pentagon, which still believed that a counter-insurgency doctrine could succeed and wanted longer to weaken the Taliban in the field.

By the time talks between US and Taliban representatives began, Obama's clear signals about ending the war had begun to erode any Taliban interest in negotiating. Karzai and ISI, each demanding a place at the table but with opposing agendas, busied themselves – by Coll's account – sabotaging the talks. Holbrooke, meanwhile, had died after collapsing in Clinton's office; his last words reportedly were, "You've got to stop this war in Afghanistan."

While Australia rates few mentions in Coll's narrative, his account helps to explain the limitations on our role. Our special forces had joined the fight against Al Qaeda when it began in October

2001 and were withdrawn when that phase of the conflict ended in 2002. They were redrafted in 2005 as the Taliban resurged, and "assigned", with the Dutch at first, to Uruzgan Province. Before our departure from Uruzgan in December 2013, Australia had become the tenth-largest troop contributor to the NATO-led coalition and a significant aid donor.

In Uruzgan the mission was demanding. It was also high-risk: forty-two Australian soldiers died, and civilian aid work could only be done amid strong security. Through political, military and diplomatic channels, we endeavoured to contribute at high policy levels in Washington and Islamabad, with the fifty coalition partners in Brussels, and as a member of the group of special representatives that Holbrooke had put together. But while we were influential in Uruzgan and had good access in Washington, Kabul and Islamabad, Coll makes clear that much of what was playing out in those capitals was beyond our capacity to influence. And the well-known differences within and between Washington's "stovepipes" made the policy-level management of our role in Afghanistan more difficult.

Coll concludes on a rueful note: while Obama announced in December 2014 that America's longest war was "coming to a responsible end", a year later it started again – this time against Islamic State and its affiliates. Back, that is, where it began.

Ric Smith

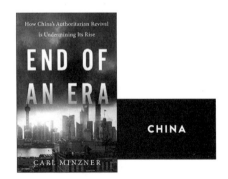

End of an Era: How China's Authoritarian Revival Is Undermining Its Rise
Carl Minzner
Oxford University Press

A cursory glance at China today hardly seems to bear out the pessimism of the subtitle of Carl Minzner's *End of an Era*.

Indeed, by many measures, objective and subjective, China seems on the crest of a mighty wave.

China's economy, still expanding at a robust pace according to official figures, remains on track to overtake that of the United States in about ten years. In Xi Jinping, China has its most determined leader in generations – in abject comparison to Donald Trump, perhaps the most wayward, ill-disciplined US president in the nation's history.

While former Chinese leader Deng Xiaoping once offered the dictum "hide your capacities and bide your time", Xi's China has no intention of maintaining a low profile. At home, the ruling Chinese Communist Party (CCP) shouts its self-professed strength and the vitality of its system from the rooftops, its voice made louder by democratic disarray around the world.

Abroad, Xi is promoting what he calls the "China solution". We've seen the future, Chinese leaders say, and it's an efficient, made-to-last authoritarian state built in our successful image. Such is the outward confidence in China that some speculate Beijing is aiming to take Taiwan in time for the centenary of the founding of the CCP in 2021.

Minzner drives his book headlong into this narrative of ascendancy. Wisely, he doesn't proclaim that China will fail because it has turned its back on any notion of becoming a Western-style democracy. He argues, more persuasively, that the CCP's China is heading dangerously backwards because of its refusal to adapt single-party rule to creative reforms rooted in Chinese history and an increasingly complex market economy.

Minzner's book has a number of commendable qualities. At the risk of being gratuitously impolite about the academy, it is worth pointing out that Minzner is an all-too-rare example of a scholar willing to put his profession's literary strictures aside and write in clear prose. It goes without saying that his clarity helps him make his case.

Minzner is far from alone in believing that China under Xi has regressed politically. The incremental institutionalisation of political norms over thirty years – term limits, a designated successor for the top job, the partial depoliticisation of the bureaucracy (based on loose notions of separating the Party from the state), and a grab bag of bottom-up reforms giving greater space to the law and the media – are being cast aside. In their place, Xi has centralised power in his inner circle; cracked down on activist lawyers and journalists; and extended the CCP's extra-legal tentacles, used in anti-corruption probes, to cover anyone on a state salary. Deng's notion of a separation of Party and state, hazy but nonetheless real, has gone out the window.

Minzner describes such changes compellingly, as have many of the expanding tribe of China-watching pessimists in recent years. But he takes his argument one crucial step further: not only are what he calls China's "counter-reforms" retrograde, they are also destined to fail in building a strong, stable China.

Xi's China, by unwinding the myriad policies that the CCP has had in place since the early 1980s to build political accountability, resolve disputes and allow scope for everything from complaints against government to genuine spiritual succour, is making the country less, not more, secure. Minzner writes that the CCP, in the process of

locking down the political system, is radicalising both the state and society, almost certainly setting up an almighty clash in the future. This is not a simple showdown between pro-Party and pro-democracy forces – it is a debilitating, violent explosion of large sections of the population, angry at the governing elite.

With no off-ramp, these mounting tensions make the CCP ever more reliant on reinforcing a nativist ethno-nationalism to buttress its governing legitimacy. In turn, the CCP has more and more reason to deploy China's military might overseas, in places such as Taiwan, to distract from growing problems at home.

All of this has happened, by the way, not in response to an economic downturn but during an economic expansion. Imagine how the system might respond when the economy goes into a slump, as it inevitably will at some stage.

Sometimes, Minzner has a tendency to throw everything into the mix to buttress his argument. Confucius made a comeback long before Xi took over leadership of the CCP, for example. And while the state sector has been strengthened under Xi, no Chinese leader has ever envisaged anything but a central role for the government in the economy.

It is true that Xi has accumulated more power in his office than any leader since Deng, and has been happy to throw out evolving norms when it suited him. But Minzner both overestimates how rosy things were under Deng and underestimates the dangers that surrounded Xi when he came to power. After all, two of Xi's ambitious rivals – Bo Xilai, the CCP chief in Chongqing, and Zhou Yongkang, who presided over the state security apparatus and the oil industry – white-anted Xi before he took over in 2012. If we believe the state media, the pair were plotting a coup to prevent Xi taking on the leadership of the CCP. Talk about challenging the party's norms! If that account is even half-true, it goes a long way to explaining Xi's brutality towards his opponents, real and imagined, on coming to office.

Minzner gives an extensive and useful account of the long processes of democratisation in South Korea and Taiwan in an effort to distinguish their development from that of China. In both places, activists battled for years to build up civil society and legal institutions, which ensured that, when formal elections were finally allowed, the system had ballast beyond the results. Minzner makes an excellent point here – far from allowing the sinews of broader political participation to develop, as happened in South Korea and Taiwan, Xi's China is shutting them down. Yet strangely, Minzner all but ignores another factor in this equation: the enormous US influence in Seoul and Taipei, and its relative absence in Beijing.

I also wonder whether Minzner, in building his gloomy account, underestimates the solidity and deep roots of the Chinese bureaucracy. It is true, as he writes, that China's technocratic sheen is fading, but it is far from gone. In Nanjing recently, a Chinese professor vented to me one minute about Xi's abolition of term limits, and then marvelled at the skill of his recent reshuffle of government ministries the next. The lesson for him was that Xi, and the system, could still function at a high level despite the frigid political climate.

Can the technocrats stand up to the ethno-nationalist wave threatening to swamp them? Will China's famed pragmatism survive the CCP's renewed effort to politicise every corner of public and economic life? Will Xi's acolytes really advocate war against Taiwan, as a kind of centennial gift for the CCP?

On the last point, count me sceptical. An invasion of Taiwan, or even a blockade, would be so risky on so many levels that it is hard to see Xi green-lighting it.

On the other big questions, Minzner is pessimistic. I find myself agreeing with much of this book, even as I wish I didn't.

Richard McGregor

Clashing over Commerce: A History of US Trade Policy
Douglas A. Irwin
University of Chicago Press

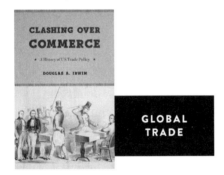

The world was surprised in 2016 by the election of New York property developer Donald J. Trump to the White House over Democrat establishment figure Hillary Clinton. Trump had never held elected office and had no fixed political allegiances, identifying as a Democrat in the 1980s before running as a Republican – albeit as a self-styled anti-establishment "outsider". To be fair, Clinton had also switched sides, starting her life as Republican (a so-called "Goldwater girl", supporting conservative presidential candidate Barry Goldwater in 1964) before becoming a Democrat and part of a political dynasty.

Perhaps less surprising was candidate Trump's message in support of trade protectionism and isolationism, which helped him to secure the nomination and the election. This stance was also taken by left-winger Bernie Sanders in the Democratic primaries, forcing Clinton to reconsider her support for the Trans-Pacific Partnership (TPP) as she began to realise how much free trade was on the nose in the American electorate.

Trump ran very hard against free trade agreements – particularly the North American Free Trade Agreement and the TPP – claiming that China and other foreign powers were taking advantage of the United States through these "lousy" deals, which, as a successful businessman, he could renegotiate. Politically, this was aimed at the blue-collar industrial swing states, which eschewed Clinton and the "Corporate Democrats" and gave Trump the electoral college votes to get him to the White House. Hillary offered them lectures on misogyny and racism; Trump offered them tariff protection. Neither is going to help them in the long run, but tariff protection might help Trump – again – in 2020.

As president, Trump has upset financial markets and US trading partners by engaging in trade policy erratically via Twitter. He announced a "trade war" with major tariff hikes in steel and aluminium, targeting China, Japan, South Korea, Mexico, Brazil and the European Union. He then abruptly suspended some of the tariffs for China (and gave exemptions to Australia) to announce a trade "peace in our time".

The on-again, off-again approach has the world reeling, especially given the Trump administration's obsession with bilateral trade deficits rather than the global stability of the world trading system.

But the temptation to throw the switch to populism didn't begin with Trump. It has a long history. That's the theme of a magnificent account of US trade policy, *Clashing over Commerce*, by renowned scholar Douglas A. Irwin. Like Australia's battles over free trade and protection at the dawn of federation, the United States has grappled with this policy question since its Founding Fathers won independence from the British Crown in 1776.

Irwin explains that US independence was declared the same year Adam Smith published his anti-mercantilist treatise *The Wealth of Nations*, and the Founding Fathers were very much acquainted with Smith's support for free trade. But the fledging colony had a problem – lack of revenue – and needed the revenue-raising aspects of protection. The nation's first treasury secretary, Alexander Hamilton, was sceptical of tariffs because they sheltered inefficient and productive enterprises, and led to consumer price increases, which encouraged smuggling and eroded government revenue. Hence Hamilton opted for bounties, or state payments to producers, over tariffs. He later clashed with Thomas Jefferson, who opposed government intervention and advocated free commerce, as the new nation navigated its way through trade wars, the British Empire's dominance over world trade, and literal wars between Britain and France.

Eventually, the debate over trade policy, as in all countries, was captured by sectional and regional interests. These divisions led to the Civil War: the manufacturing interests in the North preferred protection, and the agrarian, slave-owning states of the South preferred free trade. In fact, until the early twentieth century the Republican Party – the party of Abraham Lincoln, the president who abolished slavery – was largely protectionist in outlook, and the Southern-based Democratic Party, which wanted to keep the cost advantages of slavery in cotton, sugar and textile exports, was mainly for free trade.

According to Irwin, the Great Depression reignited tensions on the topic. In response to the high unemployment rate, Congress passed the *Hawley–Smoot Tariff Act*, which raised tariffs and caused an unprecedented decline in world trade, worsening labour-market conditions. This was partly as the tariff act encouraged trade retaliation by other nations, and led to initiatives such as the 1932 Ottawa Agreement, which restored British imperial preference by reducing tariffs for Commonwealth countries and jacking up tariffs for those outside it (so benefiting Canada and Australia and penalising Argentina). In the end, it took the New Deal and World War II to shake the effects of *Hawley–Smoot* from the world trading system.

Following World War II, the global trading system was created on a more liberal footing. After a stumble with the stillborn International Trade Organization, the General Agreement on Tariffs and Trade was set up to guide the world economy through a reduction of tariffs based on reciprocity. In this era, the United States was largely a force for liberalism, with the rounds of multilateral trade negotiations – notably the Kennedy Round, under

President John F. Kennedy – culminating in the Uruguay Round almost thirty years later, which led to the establishment of the World Trade Organization (WTO) in 1995.

However, it was around the time of the WTO's creation that the rise of the anti-globalisation movement became noticeable, epitomised in the "Battle for Seattle" WTO protests in 1999. Free trade was seen, rightly or wrongly, as responsible for the loss of American jobs, increasing economic inequality and environment degradation. The party positions became reversed, with the Democrats worried about free trade and the Republicans more sceptical of protection; this matched the changing political geography, as the Republicans dominated the South, and the Democrats the North. The decline of US blue-collar wages and employment was conveniently blamed on trade with Japan, then Mexico, and now China, and on immigration, rather than on the erosion of labour-market protection and the impact of technological change.

Today, the US political parties are in flux on trade policy, with the left, led by figures such as Sanders, outflanking the "Corporate Wall Street" Democrats represented by Clinton, and Trump outsmarting establishment Grand Old Party types and running a populist line. Both parties have their schisms over free trade versus protectionism, but these are part of a greater debate over inequality and the role of the United States in international affairs. And as fiery as these debates about trade policy are, they are nothing compared to debates about race and immigration.

What will happen next? There's now trade peace with China, but that could change at any time. Trump could win in 2020 by having a few high-profile corporations keep open a plant or two in Michigan that may have otherwise gone to China or Mexico, and then taking credit for the falling unemployment rate in the United States (which is, in fact, largely thanks to the efforts of Janet Yellen and her team at the Federal Reserve). Free trade could, rightly or wrongly, take the blame – or the credit – for the re-election of a candidate who seemed not so long ago to be a most unlikely president.

Tim Harcourt

**North Korea: The Country
We Love to Hate**
Loretta Napoleoni
UWA Publishing

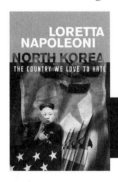

N orth Korea is a nation that, until recently, few chose to study. General perceptions of the North are largely shaped by the media and popular culture, which tend to fixate on its bizarre, menacing and sensational aspects, giving little consideration to its strategic interests. Opportunities to visit are limited, and casual or even formal encounters with North Koreans overseas are difficult to come by. Now that the country is dominating global headlines, there is, understandably, a lot of interest in figuring out who exactly Kim Jong-un is, what North Korea is really like and how this small, poor nation has become such a threat to international security.

For those curious about this seemingly opaque country, even a cursory inquiry quickly reveals an incredibly complex, multi-actor, geopolitical game that has been playing out not just since the Korean Peninsula was arbitrarily split at the end of World War II, but for centuries, as major powers fought for influence over Korean territory. An attempt to comprehend North Korea in isolation from that history leaves large gaps in understanding about the country's motivations, perceptions of threat, strategic interests, allies and adversaries, and behaviours. Delving into this broader context can be a daunting task.

Loretta Napoleoni's *North Korea: The Country We Love to Hate* claims to reject the stereotypical portrayal of North Korea as the "ultimate dystopian society" and instead to provide a "dispassionate picture of the Democratic People's Republic of Korea while seeking to unveil why and how it has survived against all odds". It includes a series of brief, accessible narratives that seemingly illuminate the made-for-television battle for hearts and minds between Kim and Donald Trump over North Korea's pursuit of a nuclear deterrent against the United States. Those who know very little about the country are whisked on a whirlwind tutorial. But this approach is problematic.

Early on, Napoleoni states that her book will steer clear of common generalisations in regard to North Korea. However, many of her conclusions fall back on simplistic and Orientalist assumptions. She suggests that because of the fates that befell Iraq and Libya, North Korea will never give up its nukes, and promises of economic cooperation are ineffective in convincing it to dismantle its nuclear weapons. While I would agree that economic incentives alone will never convince North Korea to venture down the path of denuclearisation, there are broader strategic reasons for this, not only the paranoia of ending up as another toppled regime.

North Korea's nuclear program provides not only a deterrent capability, protecting it against attack from outside forces, but also a feeling of pride and prestige. This helps to stave off internal opposition, build a sense of strategic parity with the big powers and establish superiority over South Korea. But there is little discussion in Napoleoni's account of North Korea's strategic interests, or even a definition of what denuclearisation of the Korean Peninsula means – not to mention how that relates to political negotiations with the United States and other key adversaries, and why the thinking that the United States could simply buy North Korea off was wrong to begin with.

North Korea's stance has always been that denuclearisation of the Korean Peninsula (that is, not only of North Korea) is contingent on the elimination of US "hostile policy": North Korea's political, military and economic concerns would need to be addressed with a long-term plan of action. This would include the lifting of economic sanctions, but also such measures as a peace treaty to formally end the Korean War; some common understanding of the role of the US military on the Korean Peninsula, including in local military exercises; and moves towards normalising relations with the United States. Essentially, it would take a fundamental change in North Korea's political relationship with its adversaries for it to exit its nuclear program.

While North Korea's view of denuclearisation is a complex subject, it is at the heart of where negotiations between the United States and the Democratic People's Republic of Korea have been stalling. Napoleoni's simplistic account provides little understanding of the nuance of this impasse. Statements such as "So far, North Korea has succeeded because it is unpredictable" reflect a Western bias that North Korea is unknowable. Those who have studied North Korea, and I count myself among them, would argue the exact opposite – that the North's actions and reactions align very closely with its strategic interests, provided we understand what those interests are.

Jenny Town

Correspondence

"Can Australia Fight Alone?"
by Andrew Davies

Tim Costello

Andrew Davies, in his piece "Can Australia Fight Alone?" (Australian Foreign Affairs 2, February 2018), offers some critical observations about the Australian government's plan to bolster military capability, in particular the intention to invest heavily in local weapons production, and an ambitious new goal for Australia to become a major arms exporter.

Davies astutely identifies some of the political and moral hazards this strategy entails, but his principal concerns relate to the efficacy, efficiency, costs and benefits. He doubts that anything approaching self-sufficiency can be achieved, and argues convincingly that such a build-up is unlikely to produce the economic benefits touted by the government.

This debate comes in the context of dramatic changes unfolding in the global and regional strategic environment, in which the prospect of US disengagement from Asia and the rise of Chinese economic and military power loom especially large.

Obviously, no Australian government can ignore such dramatic changes, actual or prospective. Yet it does not automatically follow that an increase in military capability is the best or only response available. Nor does it make sense to conceive of security only in military terms, or to consider militarisation as the best or only set of tools to protect the security and economic interests of Australia and our neighbours. The financial cost involved is daunting – we rarely talk of a spending commitment in the hundreds of billions – and the economic benefits are unlikely to materialise. As Davies notes, the defence industry constitutes a very small element of the total Australian economy, and is comparatively poor as a revenue generator or a jobs creator.

Defence production can be highly profitable for the contractors, and a major part of their sales pitch is potential economic, and therefore political, gains. However, the same pitch is made to many countries, and the balance of bargaining power often tilts towards the contractors. This is especially true in Australia, where competitive federalism sees state governments offering extra incentives in the hope of attracting manufacturing jobs. The Victorian government, for example, has been betting heavily on what it terms the "pivot to defence" as the state's strategic response to the shutdown of car manufacturing. Yet it was recently outbid by Queensland for a $5 billion armoured vehicle contract awarded to the German contractor Rheinmetall.

That amount alone – about 1 per cent of what the government plans to spend on defence over the next decade – is more than the total annual budget for all of Australia's diplomatic and development programs combined.

This goes to the heart of what is wrong with the government's strategy, even beyond the immense moral and political risks, and the poor economic cost–benefit ratio. The strategic approach mistakes military spending for the thing it is meant to achieve: stability and security in our region. Just as we can pump money into medical care with little gain in health outcomes, we can also throw vast sums at military defence without effectively improving our security – if we fail to pay adequate attention to the factors that promote insecurity in the first place.

Insecurity in our region is not exclusively the product of the shifting balance between China and the United States, or of the military expansion and modernisation of regional powers concomitant to their economic growth. Insecurity at the human level is driven by poverty, lack of economic opportunity, poor health, lack of services, climate change, frequent and intense natural disasters, environmental degradation, corruption, failures in governance, weak institutions, transnational crime, and the threat of violence and conflict, often fuelled by ethnic or religious tensions.

Yet the Australian government's strategic choice appears to focus almost wholly on military defence, pulling back from its engagement with regional partners by adopting a minimalist approach to regional development and partnerships. Our budget for overseas development has now fallen to 0.22 per cent of gross national income, a low figure not previously seen, and one that puts us well into the lower half of OECD countries, despite having one of its highest income levels and the much-vaunted quarter-century of continuous economic growth. The reduction in aid, and the chopping and changing of commitments, has bruised Australia's reputation as a reliable partner. It has also undermined our efforts at building a stable region.

AusAID, the specialised agency that formerly managed Australia's aid program, has been subsumed into DFAT, with a considerable loss of both development and management expertise; decision-making has increasingly shifted to heads of mission. DFAT operates under resource constraints, with Australia fielding a small diplomatic presence compared to other OECD countries. The Australian aid program still achieves a great deal, and the potential exists to revive it, but a generational opportunity to achieve genuine transformative progress, to the benefit of those in the Pacific region as well as to Australia's security and prosperity, has been lost.

Australian politicians, when they think about the Pacific at all, still tend either to dismiss the region's challenges as insoluble or unimportant, or to think in colonialist terms. Our approach is essentially unchanged from the post-independence period. Despite concern over China's growing regional influence, there has been surprisingly little energy put into thinking through what an effective framework for regional partnership might look like. When that effort finally comes, it will undoubtedly require serious investment.

Like Andrew Davies, I can only be sceptical about the supposed economic benefits of Australian militarisation. I do not think that all-round armament enhances global security. I am worried that an orientation to arms exports will create greater risk of violent conflict, and it seems unlikely that any Australian government can guarantee that Australian weapons will not contribute to dirty wars and serious human rights abuses.

But I also believe it is mistaken to consider defence in isolation from the other challenges we face, or from the other policy tools at our disposal. Australian policy and resource allocation is distorted, and pays far too little attention to either diplomacy or development, and especially to the potential benefits of a genuinely effective aid program. The government's 2017 Foreign Policy White Paper was another missed opportunity to recognise aid as a core asset of Australia's foreign policy.

Recently, the government did some modelling of how a further $400 million cut to the aid program might be implemented, though the proposed cut was quickly denied. I was pleased to read one media account that said my predictable voice was not the only one raised in outrage. Indeed, some within the "defence establishment" were quoted as considering such a move foolish and self-defeating.

Many in the aid community have altruistic impulses and feel uncomfortable about the suggestion that Australian aid, besides helping overcome poverty and injustice, is in our national interest. Those concerned with Australian foreign and security policy have equally tended to show discomfort with advocating publicly for anything beyond our own strategic defence. This is a binary divide we can no longer afford. Rather than hurtling headlong towards a cripplingly expensive, ineffective and morally hazardous armaments binge, isn't it time we developed a more integrated, nuanced and sophisticated approach to securing stability in our region?

Tim Costello, chief advocate of World Vision Australia

Jim Molan

n "Can Australia Fight Alone?" Andrew Davies acknowledges increasing strategic uncertainty, but concludes that the only credible scenario in which Australia might need "greater self-reliance" is extensive operations in our near neighbourhood, focusing entirely on war with Indonesia. If we conduct operations far from our shores, we will invariably be positioned alongside our major allies, so can rely on them. As a result, says Davies, "we should resist the push for extra defence spending". "Our armed forces," he claims, "can do everything they are likely to be able to do, whether in coalition operations far from home – in which case, we're likely to be alongside our major suppliers – or operating alone in our own backyard, which tends to be less demanding, at least in terms of sophisticated capabilities."

This is a comforting thought, but like so much Australian strategic analysis, it is deeply flawed, and dangerous to the independence and perhaps even existence of this nation. In the great tradition of hope-based strategic thought, it focuses on the past rather than the present and the future.

For the last seventy-five years Australia has had no need for independent strategic analysis because of our relationship with our great and powerful ally the United States. That has now changed. The emergence of "four nations and an ideology" (Russia, Iran, China and North Korea plus Islamism) and the relative decline in US power means that little from the recent past can be carried into our strategic future. Davies' piece reflects a belief that, for the foreseeable future, Australia will be able to choose the conditions under which it goes to war, a luxury referred to as "conflicts of choice". This outlook assumes that only events in what Davies calls the near neighbourhood will require a significant military response from Australia, and that threatening events will only occur at a manageable rate of one at a time.

The Australian Defence Force has grown to become what it is as a result of the activities that it has been asked to conduct, a certain amount of replacement philosophy (if we have fighters now, we must buy fighters again) and the limits imposed by financial constraints. This has worked in the past because Australia has not been tested in a military sense, and therefore we may consider what we have at the moment as military perfection.

Davies' willingness to be so specific in relation to the likelihood and nature of future war is breathtaking. He says, definitively, that we don't have to spend more on defence because he has predicted the future, and the future will be like the past. He may indeed be right, but he could also be very, very wrong.

What he does not address is that if 2 per cent of GDP spent on defence was the aim of most "Western nations" for the last seventy-five years, when the United States dominated the world, why would 2 per cent continue to be an appropriate defence spend when the US no longer dominates the world, its relative military power has diminished and other nations are challenging the status quo?

Davies maintains that "operating alone in our own backyard ... tends to be less demanding, at least in terms of sophisticated capabilities". Why would his supposed war with Indonesia be less demanding in terms of capabilities? There is no logic in this, only wishful thinking. And why would Davies think that we would only ever have to conduct one military operation at a time? Is it beyond reason that Australia may have deployed forces far from home alongside our major ally, and then have to provide smaller forces in other regions for various tasks, as well as build up domestic forces for a third developing threat?

Australia should welcome the rise of regional nations from a position of strength, not as a supplicant, hoping that we will be treated well. What this nation lacks (and what only government can provide) is a cohesive national security policy that addresses the current strategic environment and is put into effect through a defence strategy. Such a policy would define what is to be achieved by the ADF and allocate resources in a general sense (whether 2 per cent of GDP, less or more). In essence, it would tell *what* Australia has to do. This should be complemented by one or more operational concepts (with much more detail than the classified Australian Joint Operational Concept) and endorsed by government, which would allow us to say *how* Australia will do whatever is required, if Australia needs to fight alone, where it might need to fight, the way it might fight, and what we need to enable it to fight. We as a nation could decide if we are prepared to fund this effort, and if we are not, we understand the risk. Accepting Davies' view that we are doing enough now is an easy way out of any rigorous thinking.

Australians think they are well defended because of the responsible actions of the present government: 2 per cent of GDP soon; $200 billion over the next decade in equipment; competent performance by elements of the ADF in recent conflicts. But there is no way Australians can really know if they are well defended except if government develops an open policy and a strategy that explains the risk. We need to understand the cost required to meet a strategy, as well as the consequences of not meeting it. This is the only way our society can decide whether to accept that risk, and it stresses the need for government to exercise responsible leadership on defence. And remember, deterrence depends on an opponent knowing your capability.

Davies seems to think that we cannot defend ourselves independently. That is not true. It is not impossible. We may have to do it, and should never rule it out. Australia has enormous latent defence potential, and all we need is resolve, and the time to do it. We have the riches. Australians make an unconscious decision not to provide funds to defend ourselves because we are fed a superficial line that we do not need to. I think we may need to, and I believe that we can, but only government can ultimately decide the issue.

Jim Molan, Liberal Senator for New South Wales
and former major general in the Australian Army

Innes Willox and Kate Louis

I n "Can Australia Fight Alone?" Andrew Davies raises several important issues in relation to self-reliance and investing in the defence sector.

It is critical that policymakers get our level of self-reliance right – the stakes are high. Australia has paid the price in the past, with the Collins-class submarine program, for an insufficient level of sovereign rights for maintenance and support.

Before the federal government announced its plan to focus on Australian investment in the 2016 Defence Industry Policy Statement, Australia largely purchased equipment from overseas, leading to a significant decline in domestic industry capability. Until recently, Australia was the only comparable developed nation that did not leverage its large and powerful defence spend to focus on economic prosperity, and use it to create wealth and a skilled workforce for future generations.

Our close economic and strategic partners, including the United States, the United Kingdom, Canada and our European allies, fiercely support and promote their domestic defence industries and invest heavily in defence-related research and development. The federal government's recent changes to invest in a sovereign Australian defence industry are a once-in-a-generation opportunity to develop our national security posture, to further build our defence industry and to create a high-tech manufacturing industry. These changes depart from the simple drive to buy everything from overseas. They have received bipartisan support for clear and obvious reasons.

Davies is correct that we will never build all our military equipment here, nor would it be sensible to do so – and the obvious example is fighter jets. There will be many other examples where we continue, very sensibly, to buy our equipment from overseas. But a balance is required.

While everyone in industry would agree with buying modern aircraft from (mainly US) production lines, we must be in a position to maintain and repair them. Key items, such as F/A-18 engines (of all types), are repaired here, which has also created the capability to repair Abrams tank engines. Local repair in the latter case improved availability, serviceability and reliability. This was done through selected technology transfer and creation of local industrial infrastructure, skills and capabilities, supported by either a local or a US supply chain. It has helped support Australia to become a regional hub for Joint Strike Fighter maintenance.

Will we ever go it alone for everything, everywhere? Highly unlikely. But we must invest in the core industrial capabilities we will need to build upon in the event of conflict, supported by coalition partners where need be. We must recognise that demands placed on a coalition partner's industrial base during a conflict may mean we are given lower priority than expected. We need to anticipate these risks, and ensure we can step up and build, modify, repair and upgrade quickly if need be.

With clear policies that focus on defence capability first and seek to maximise Australian content, it is possible to get the balance right between ensuring operational availability and increasing local content, while avoiding the overreach that concerns Davies. The strengthened Australian Industry Capability Program, announced by Minister Christopher Pyne on 29 June 2017, does not mandate Australian content, but creates a positive environment for competitive Australian businesses to be considered in the context of major purchases. As a direct result of the federal government's policies, Australian industry is increasingly involved in the huge acquisition programs, including armoured vehicles and shipbuilding.

Our manufacturing sector is strong and vibrant, employing almost 900,000 Australians, who make up around 7.3 per cent of our total workforce. Similarly, Austrade estimates that the defence industry employs around 27,000 Australians and, while there is no specific ABS data on defence exports, the federal government estimates that they amount to between $1.5 billion and $2.5 billion a year.

We have a proud manufacturing record both in defence and more broadly. Thales Bushmaster Protected Mobility Vehicles, CEAFAR phased array radar, Austal ships and BAE Nulka missile decoys are world-beaters in terms of our Australian capabilities and export potential. Sustainment and maintenance of the Collins-class submarine is now regarded as a core sovereign capability. The federal government is looking to build on these successes, opening up many opportunities for Australian businesses across the supply chain.

Our manufacturers are quickly evolving from old-world factories to modern, high-technology, research-linked operations that are competitive and focused on global markets. They are embracing the digitisation imperative. Defence is as advanced as any sector in leading these trends.

Strong and prosperous countries invest in their domestic defence industries. With the right policy settings, leadership and investment we can create an even more successful Australian defence industry, with the security and economic benefits that will go with it.

Innes Willox, chief executive of the Australian Industry Group, and Kate Louis,
executive director of the Australian Industry Group Defence Council

Andrew Davies responds

The diversity of responses to my article reveals the competing factors to be resolved when formulating strategic policy and allocating national resources.

I agree with much of what Tim Costello writes. Like him, I think that even a modest increase in our development and diplomatic resources in the Pacific region would offer a greater return in terms of security than further boosting the defence budget. And Costello is right to point to a Pacific policy that does not give sufficient weight to developing our regional partnerships – especially in a world where China is exerting substantially more influence. In that context I'd suggest we might also usefully put some thinking into our relationships in the Indian Ocean region.

Costello is also correct that increasing the number of armaments in the world could lead to reduced, rather than increased, security. There will always be a moral dilemma associated with arms exports, though some sales are less likely to be destabilising than others. The main impact of sales to developed countries such as Canada, Japan, the United Kingdom and the United States is replacing other suppliers in the marketplace, rather than increasing militarisation. But selling into markets in less stable parts of the world, or to governments whose concept of human rights is not attuned to ours, is far more fraught. It's an obvious slippery slope when increasing defence exports becomes a driver of investment in the industry.

Having spent a lot of time over the past fifteen years arguing with Jim Molan, I would almost have been disappointed if he hadn't responded to my piece. His characteristically robust reply has some merit; there is little doubt that our defence forces could do more if we spent more on equipping and supporting them. More capability is indeed more capability. But spending on additional defence capability comes at an opportunity cost to other elements of national effort. And, harking back to Costello's remarks, we should only spend more on defence if it offers better returns than other avenues of investment.

To simplify my position – though not to the extent that Molan does in places – I argue that self-sufficiency is practically unachievable, that pursuit of it is prohibitively expensive and that it is unnecessary in the most likely future we face. I think my article makes a cogent case that the arguments suggesting that increased defence spending pays for itself by building up the economy are deeply flawed. So the basic difference between my position and Molan's is the extent of the security insurance we think can be purchased cost-effectively through defence spending. He is right that I limited my ambition for the Australian Defence Force to scenarios in which we fight far from home alongside coalition partners, or closer to home on our own. Molan wants to be able to do both at once, and to be able to conduct independent expeditionary operations far from home.

At one level there is no argument: a certain amount of defence spending would allow for Molan's vision, and the increased spending would retire additional security risk. But there will always be scenarios that could overwhelm whatever preparations we make, and the size of the Australian population and economy limits the size and sophistication of the force we can raise and reasonably afford. I suspect we would still find ourselves well short of being able to fight a significant power far from home without support – in which case the question becomes: why would we invest in the ability to do so? Lest there be any doubt, consider the problem of facing a nuclear-armed adversary alone. As has been the case for the entire modern history of our country, our status as (at best) a middle power limits what we can reasonably aspire to do.

The ability to do more, and to conduct more concurrent operations, would cost much more than the current level of around 2 per cent of GDP. I made a case for some reasonable future scenarios, which Molan takes issue with, stating that my "willingness to be so specific in relation to the likelihood and nature of future war is breathtaking". His solution – without any apparent sense of contradiction – is the development of a "cohesive national security policy that [says] *how* Australia will do whatever is required, if Australia needs to fight alone, where it might need to fight, the way it might fight, and what we need to enable it to fight". It seems it is permissible to specify the nature and location of future conflicts, provided the answer is more, rather than less, defence spending. Ultimately there is no single right answer, but spending more to be able to do more is only sometimes valid, and Molan and I differ on where to draw the line.

The industry-sector response to my piece from Innes Willox and Kate Louis makes one point on which we can certainly agree. Namely, the ADF will always need local-based industry support to maintain and repair its equipment, as well as to supply a wide range of other goods and services. It's worth noting that the authors' given example – the Collins-class submarine – is a direct result of Australia's last concerted effort to build a domestic defence industry. The outcome was a uniquely Australian platform that required a uniquely configured support framework, which was subsequently mismanaged. But jet fighters – which we're told "everyone in industry" agrees can be safely sourced from offshore – require pretty much the same support anywhere, so we can safely look to the world market to provide the necessary services locally.

In fact, I'm pleased to learn that "everyone" agrees about the wisdom of buying fast jets from elsewhere, because that makes my fundamental point. If we continue to rely on external support for our air combat capability, there is no compelling case for building self-sufficiency in other parts of the force structure. Given the centrality of air power to modern warfare, the existence of a consensus on outsourcing its development and supply is telling. Together, the Collins-class submarines and the RAAF fast jets show that building defence equipment in Australia is neither necessary nor sufficient to ensure that the ADF has high-performing equipment.

Willox and Louis' response makes familiar pleas for more government support of the defence sector, but does not present the business case for doing so. We read, for example, that "Australia is the only comparable developed nation that did not leverage its large and powerful defence spend to focus on economic prosperity, and use it to create wealth and a skilled workforce for future generations". I explain in my article why I think that is the case, and why I think that is a smart strategy based on comparative advantage. Just because everyone else does it, it doesn't follow that it would be smart for us to – in fact, the converse could well be true.

The rational approach to defence spending is to outlay additional resources only when they will be justified by the return. To get behind a push for more local defence industry investment, I'd need to see more than a questionable assertion about "the security and economic benefits" that will allegedly follow.

Andrew Davies, lecturer in the Strategic and Defence Studies Centre
at the Australian National University

"The Pivot to Chaos"
by Michael Wesley

Peter Jennings

n an age of parallel universes it's possible that Michael Wesley visits a different Asia from the one I do. In his essay "The Pivot to Chaos" (Australian Foreign Affairs 2, February 2018), Wesley suggests that Asian societies are something of a "Trump-muted zone", that "there is resigned acceptance that China will become the dominant power in Asia" and that Australia needs to urgently rethink our strategy towards our alliance with the United States and towards the region. I'm not sure any of these assessments is right, but I can agree with Wesley that this is important stuff, and that Canberra needs to shake off its autumn complacency and get to grips with our changing strategic environment.

Let's go to the disagreements first. Wesley and I are dealing in generalities, but my engagements with Asian policy and strategic thinkers suggest that there is deep concern about Donald Trump. The worry is not, as Wesley suggests, because Trump has made "so profound a break with America's animating principles" of engagement with Asia. Rather, it's the "look, Ma, no hands" approach that Trump takes to steering the United States. He may bring peace to the Korean Peninsula, but in jumping the shark – backwards and blindfolded – Trump could easily take us to war. Whatever he achieves, we can be certain it won't be informed by a deep understanding of the past or current principles of US engagement in Asia. Unlike his predecessor, the president isn't hidebound by book learning.

If anything, Asian assessments of Barack Obama are more damning than those of Trump. It was Obama who made the Trans-Pacific Partnership the centrepiece of his Asian policy and whose distaste for engaging with Congress led to the treaty not being ratified. It was Obama who botched completely America's response to China's annexation of the South China Sea, dismissing it as a spat over rocks and shoals, when in fact it was every bit as audacious an annexation as Russia's occupation of Crimea. It was Obama who promised to pivot but paused and prevaricated in all but the smallest of America's rebalancing efforts. This was the unpromising strategic landscape Trump inherited. Just when we needed Captain America, we got the Hulk. But while the Donald's gyrations bemuse Canberra's policymakers, the reality is that Trump has strengthened America's Asian alliances. He has spent a significant amount of time in the region, developed good relations with Japan's Shinzō Abe, India's Narendra Modi and Australia's Malcolm Turnbull and, thankfully, given China pause in its headlong opportunistic assault on that frail and quaking creature, the international rule of law.

If there is a degree of calm in Asian capitals about Trump, it's because America's regional friends and allies are judging what the United States is doing rather than worrying about the US president's relentless domestic theatre aimed at "the base". Asian leaders also realise that the biggest risk the region faces isn't the United States but China. President Xi Jinping's recentralisation of power, the unrolling of the instruments of a pervasive internal surveillance state, accompanied by rapid military growth and an assertive nationalism: this is the true cause of Asian worries about regional stability. I believe that Asian capitals understood the risks presented by a freshly re-Leninised China much faster than Australia did. But now even the most obdurate Treasury official in Canberra realises that Australia's business model – of getting rich while China grows – is broken. Economic dependence on China carries deep strategic costs.

So to Wesley's solution, and here I must confess to not quite seeing the novelty of the step he proposes. Wesley states, "The first challenge is to let go of the belief that only American primacy can ensure an acceptable regional order." How do we do this? The answer is simple: "This is where we need the United States to play a vital role in bringing about a new equilibrium in the Asia-Pacific." Aha! Only the Americans can lead us to a world where American power balances against China's and indeed any other threats to regional stability.

There is the finest shade of difference between the idea of American "primacy" and America acting as a "balancer" in the region. I don't think the idea of American primacy survived much past March 2003 and the invasion of Iraq.

For at least the last decade and a half in Asia, Australian and American policy have, under a healthy variety of governments, aimed at creating a strategic fabric in the region that balances the competing aspirations of China and its neighbours. The suggestion that Australian policy should shift to encourage America's role as a "balancer" is not new; it describes precisely what Canberra has been doing since before Alexander Downer discovered fishnet stockings. The more fundamental challenge for all of us is to ask what the region does now it's clear that China is not for balancing. The great experiment to bring China into the Western-conceived international system has failed. This is the world we are heading to at lightning pace.

Peter Jennings, executive director of the Australian Strategic Policy Institute and former deputy secretary for strategy in the department of defence

Chengxin Pan

n the debate on Australia's strategic options regarding a rising China and an uncertain United States, Michael Wesley's "The Pivot to Chaos" is a welcome intervention. There is much in his argument to agree with. With Trump in the White House, Wesley urges Australia to, like many Asian countries, adopt a less sentimental and moralistic view on US power. He rightly points out the limits of American commitment to the region, and argues that the United States' habitual display of military force has done little to deter rivals in the region; instead, it often helps motivate them to catch up.

Given the changing strategic environment of the Asia-Pacific, Wesley issues a daring and timely call for reimagining Australia's place in the region and recalibrating its foreign policy. Such reimagining is indeed long overdue. Yet his essay is short on detail as to how the reimagining may take shape, beyond an emphasis on moderating China's behaviour and convincing the United States to shift to a balancing role in the region. These are reasonable goals, but it remains unclear to me what policy adjustments Australia should make to achieve them.

In fact, I am doubtful whether Australia will make any meaningful policy adjustments at all. Wesley is certainly under no illusion that such foreign policy reimagining is going to be easy. After all, Australia hasn't been here before, "living in a region not dominated by a culturally similar ally". Still, I think his essay has not fully accounted for the magnitude of the challenge in persuading the Australian political and strategic elites to change tack.

For example, Wesley could have paid closer attention to the role of identity and discourse in shaping Australia's strategic imagination. He justifies the need to "become as unromantic about American power as our northern neighbours" on the basis of an unconventional and unpredictable president in the White House and the "relative decline of American power". But will this be sufficient for Canberra to distance itself emotionally from Washington? I very much doubt it.

Wesley carefully documents how the US strategy in Asia has revolved around three pillars: preserving alliances and strategic partnerships, strengthening regional and global institutions and rules, and projecting its military strength. However, what he briefly alludes to but neglects to dwell on is the fact that the US strategy contains a fourth element, no less important: remaking countries (particularly its allies) in the region in its own image.

This has been the gist of the concept of US alliances in the region since former president Harry Truman – Australia and Japan have been turned into not only military allies but also small versions of the United States, at least at the level of political establishment. Indeed, the Australia–US alliance is not only based on military hardware interoperability. To borrow Malcolm Turnbull's phrase, "we are joined at the hip" at so many levels: political, cultural, discursive. As such, it must take more than concern about an unpredictable US president to untie the deep romantic bond between the two countries. Australians feel romantic about American power for a reason, and for many, that reason is strong and sacrosanct.

Wesley's argument about the United States and China has not made the case for reimagining policy any easier. For instance, he assumes that the United States "provide[s] the stability that has allowed the region's astonishingly rapid development". This assumption about the benevolence of US leadership in the region, though not without merit, plays into the larger discourse about the indispensability of US global leadership. It is here that a curious contradiction emerges in his analysis. On the one hand, this belief in US leadership implies that there will be no stability without it; Wesley writes that we cannot be confident that other regional powers will be able to ensure stability, access and equality. On the other hand, without much explanation apart from the Trump factor, he urges Australia to "let go of the belief that only American primacy can ensure an acceptable regional order".

Equally, his depiction of China's rise in terms of a determined effort to confront US dominance offers little incentive for Australia to rethink its policy. If anything, the perceived China challenge would give further impetus to rallying around the United States. While China's rise no doubt poses challenges to Australia and the wider region, some acknowledgement of China's role in regional trade and cooperation on common concerns could have helped him better sell his "reimagining" message. But since there is no mention of any of these things in his essay, his sceptics would feel hard-pressed to go along with his push for Australia to be dispassionate about the power shift in the region or to reshape its US alliance.

If it is indeed true, as Wesley notes, that our future will increasingly be shaped by Beijing, not by Washington, and that a Beijing-centred regional order won't be sympathetic to our values or interests, would this be all the more reason for Australia to try to fend off that terrifying future by clinging to the United States, despite the latter now being led by "the president without a plan"? Wesley's notion of reimagining Australia's role in the Asia-Pacific is laudable and timely, but he still has a tough job to convince the sceptics why Australia should bother.

Chengxin Pan, associate professor
of international relations at Deakin University

Purnendra Jain

Michael Wesley's incisive essay "The Pivot to Chaos" captures some of the key politico-strategic developments in the post–Cold War Asia-Pacific, the role the United States has played in this, the sorts of institutions it has crafted, and how Asian nations have responded. While I agree largely with Wesley's argument, two points should be addressed: Wesley's analysis of Donald Trump and how Asian nations view the US president; and the rapid and likely history-changing events involving North Korea that have occurred since his piece was written – which Wesley failed to see coming.

Asia is not a Trump-muted zone, as Wesley has argued. The Trump presidency is as much discussed and debated in Asia as elsewhere, perhaps even more so, because while most Asian nations might accept US influence with a hint of resentment, few prefer to see a US-free Asia. Indeed, the importance of the United States has only increased since Trump became president. In my experience, not a single meeting with colleagues and researchers from Tokyo to New Delhi has ended without a deep discussion about Trump and the implications of his role and actions. The US president figures more in their conversations than ever before because Trump is an unconventional, unpredictable and idiosyncratic leader, and hence very different from his predecessors. Trump might state that a particular Asian leader is "ripping us off", but in subsequent meetings with this very same person Trump will call him a "friend". This fickleness gives rise to considerable nervousness in Asian capitals, especially among political leaders and top-ranking officials.

Many Asian leaders have travelled to the United States for meetings with Trump, and many have received him in their national capitals. It is not always clear whether this is out of respect and the convention that follows the induction of a new president into the White House, or due to anxiety about his unpredictability.

Today we are living in a world of greater uncertainty than ever before. Of course, this is not just a phenomenon caused by Trump; past American presidents have also provided plenty of surprises and shocks to partners and allies, whether it was Nixon's approach to China or Bush's unilateral intervention in Iraq. What Trump has done, though, is to double down on uncertainties through his continual tweets, often posted without clear narratives or objectives.

Tokyo, Seoul, Beijing and New Delhi are watching Washington with more vigilance than ever because of a president whose foreign policy narratives and goals are different from those of his predecessors. Wesley's point about Trump's unpredictability seems right, but to say that his predecessors demonstrated resolve and clarity is an overstatement.

In his essay Wesley does not discuss what might happen on the Korean Peninsula. North-East Asia is a potential flashpoint and one of the world's most dangerous regions as a result of the DPRK's seemingly insatiable hunger for missiles and nuclear capabilities. Yet Wesley is silent on this issue.

North Korea has not only challenged its near neighbours, such as South Korea and Japan; it has also included the mainland United States within its nuclear strike capability, sending spine-chilling strategic messages across the region and beyond. The Obama administration's policy of "strategic patience" and "contracting out" to China, in the hope of reining in North Korea's behaviour, failed utterly. Under Obama, North Korea increased its missile and nuclear capacities by conducting two nuclear tests. Other than depend on Beijing – which of course had its own interests to promote – Obama seemed helpless to push American interests, let alone those of its North-East Asian allies.

While Obama and his predecessors failed to restrain North Korea, Trump's threats of "fire and fury" and a bigger nuclear button seem to have forced Kim to consider reaching out to Washington and offering an olive branch of sorts.

Whatever the outcome of a Trump–Kim or US–DPRK meeting, Asian leaders should not be under the illusion that the United States is always there to act as a policeman and to re-engineer the world order to its advantage, as it has in the past. Uncertainties and chaos are the new normal; Trump has given this message more loudly and clearly than any past president. Asian leaders need, therefore, to get used to a more chaotic world – and to think for themselves.

Purnendra Jain, professor of Asian studies
at the University of Adelaide

Michael Wesley responds

The three responses to my essay agree with me on one thing: Australia is in the middle of a major reordering of power in its region that poses deep challenges to its traditional foreign policy settings, including its alliance with the United States. This, I argued, is not Donald Trump's doing. It was well underway before Trump took up residence in the White House – but he adds significant uncertainties and possibilities to the evolving situation.

While Peter Jennings, Chengxin Pan and Purnendra Jain make some important points, I'm not sure they've quite understood the thrust of my argument. Jennings argues that Australia has it all in hand, and has done since Alexander Downer first discovered fishnet stockings, while Pan argues that the challenge of moving away from traditional foreign policy settings is not only *not* in hand, but is beyond a country so devoted to its ally. Jain suggests it's all about North Korea's nukes.

That three acute observers disagree with me is no great surprise; that they disagree with one another more than they do with me suggests that they're interpreting what I was arguing through their own predispositions.

Peter Jennings believes I am contradicting myself when I say that we should let go of the idea that only American primacy can assure an acceptable regional order, and that the United States needs to play a vital role in finding a new equilibrium. This is because he believes I'm arguing for "a world where American power balances against China and indeed any other threats to regional stability". I'm not arguing for this at all. In fact, I couldn't disagree more with Jennings' assertion that "there is the finest shade of difference between the idea of American 'primacy' and America as a 'balancer' in the region". Primacy and balance are polar opposites, as statesmen and thinkers from Thucydides to Churchill demonstrated. Every major conflict on the European continent for the last half-millennium has been fought to avoid the primacy of a particular power and to restore the continent to a balance of power. It was not for a fine shade of difference that millions gave their lives.

"A world where American power balances against China" is not a balance – it is a bipolar standoff. It is a situation forecast by people such as Aaron Friedberg, the academic and former deputy assistant for national security affairs, in which the United States and China carve out mutually exclusive spheres of influence, marked by deepening hostility and pervasive instability. If this is the world that Jennings believes Australian foreign policy has been working towards, we should all be very worried.

The balance that I advocate us working towards is not bipolar but multi-polar. It is not about regional countries such as Australia and Japan lining up behind the United States as a single bloc to counter or contain China's power. This approach is doomed to fail. It is about significant powers around China's periphery defining their interests clearly, and being prepared to push back against China when they believe Beijing is threatening their interests. China has shown in the South China Sea that it can outmanoeuvre the United States in a situation where other countries leave the initiative to Washington. But a range of neighbours prepared to face Beijing down at multiple points around its frontiers represents a different proposition for China. Yes, the United States needs to be part of this balance, but as one of several great powers – not as the sole balancer.

Chengxin Pan agrees that Australia needs a new approach, but he doubts we can achieve it. Perhaps he would be right if I were arguing for repudiating the alliance. I am not. I am arguing for recalibrating the alliance in a way that encourages the United States to act as one of the great powers in a multipolar balance in Asia. Can we do this? I believe so, because we've shifted the alliance three times in our recent history. In 1941–42 we were prepared to act against the express wishes of our close ally, Britain, to bring our forces home from the Middle East, and we engaged with a new strategic partner, the United States, against Japan. After the Vietnam War, we completely reconstituted our defence doctrine from expeditionary to defence of our shores, while maintaining the alliance. And after the Cold War, we shifted the alliance again, basing it not only on threat prevention but also on maintenance of the global order.

I disagree with Pan that US strategy in Asia has a fourth element: "remaking countries (particularly its allies) in the region in its own image". Perhaps it may have tried this in Europe through the Marshall Plan and in Japan through its occupation, but there is no evidence for this more broadly in Asia. In fact, I would argue that the United States tolerated illiberal political regimes and heavily statist economic policies among its Asian allies to an extent it would never have done in Europe. For much of the last half-century, Washington has counted many of Asia's dictators and autocrats among its closest friends in the interests of stability.

Jain complains that I don't pay enough attention to North Korea. I don't include North Korea because my essay is about the broad geopolitics of the region. As much as Kim Jong-un would like to think he is a major player in Asia's geopolitical shifts, I'm afraid I don't agree. The North Korean problem has been with us since at least 1994, and its evolution has had little effect on the broader strategic picture.

Jain and Jennings dispute my contention that Asian elites aren't as obsessed by Donald Trump as we are. I based my argument not on impressionistic meetings but on the systematic research of my colleagues at ANU's College of Asia and the Pacific, who found a remarkable paucity of Trump news and gossip in the media among regional countries from Indonesia to India. Their essays can be found at http://asiapacific.anu.edu.au/trump-100-days.

Michael Wesley, dean of the College of Asia and the Pacific
at the Australian National University

Subscribe to Australian Foreign Affairs & save up to 28% on the cover price.

Enjoy free home delivery of the print edition and full digital access to the journal via the Australian Foreign Affairs website, iPad, iPhone and Android apps.

Forthcoming issue: Defending Australia (October 2018)

Never miss an issue. Subscribe and save.

☐ **1 year auto-renewing print and digital subscription** (3 issues) $49.99 within Australia. Outside Australia $79.99

☐ **1 year print and digital subscription** (3 issues) $59.99 within Australia. Outside Australia $99.99

☐ **1 year digital-only subscription** (3 issues) $29.99.

☐ **2 year print and digital subscription** (6 issues) $114.99 within Australia.

☐ Tick here to commence subscription with the current issue.

Give an inspired gift. Subscribe a friend.

☐ **1 year print and digital gift subscription** (3 issues) $59.99 within Australia. Outside Australia $99.99

☐ **1 year digital-only gift subscription** (3 issues) $29.99.

☐ **2 year print and digital gift subscription** (6 issues) $114.99 within Australia.

☐ Tick here to commence subscription with the current issue.

ALL PRICES INCLUDE GST, POSTAGE AND HANDLING.

*Your subscription will automatically renew until you notify us to stop. Prior to the end of your subscription period, we will send you a reminder notice.

Please turn over for subscription order form, or subscribe online at **australianforeignaffairs.com**
Alternatively, call 1800 077 514 or +61 3 9486 0288 or email **subscribe@australianforeignaffairs.com**

Back Issues ALL PRICES INCLUDE GST, POSTAGE AND HANDLING.

☐ **AFA1** ($22.99) The Big Picture

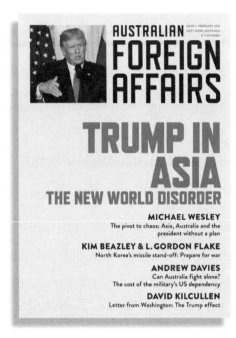

☐ **AFA2** ($22.99) Trump in Asia

PAYMENT DETAILS I enclose a cheque/money order made out to Schwartz Publishing Pty Ltd.
Or please debit my credit card (MasterCard, Visa or Amex accepted).

CARD NO.

EXPIRY DATE   /   CCV   AMOUNT $

CARDHOLDER'S NAME

SIGNATURE

NAME

ADDRESS

EMAIL   PHONE

Post or fax this form to: Reply Paid 90094, Carlton VIC 3053 **Freecall:** 1800 077 514 **or** +61 3 9486 0288
Fax: (03) 9011 6106 **Email:** subscribe@australianforeignaffairs.com **Website:** australianforeignaffairs.com
Subscribe online at australianforeignaffairs.com/subscribe

The Back Page

THE WASHINGTON CONSENSUS

What is it: A name given to the "standard package" of free-market reforms once applied to distressed economies, especially developing ones, coined by John Williamson (economist, Peterson Institute for International Economics) in 1989. His version encompassed fiscal discipline, liberalising interest and exchange rates, privatisation, deregulation, tax reform and property rights.

Who buys it: Hardly anyone, partly due to confusion over its meaning. Some critics, such as Moisés Naím (editor-in-chief, *Foreign Policy*), argue it was not from Washington and never a consensus. Others, such as Gordon Brown (former prime minister, United Kingdom), claim it was killed off by the 2008 financial crisis: "The old Washington Consensus is over," he told the G20 in 2009.

Who doesn't: Joseph Stiglitz (Nobel Prize winner, economics) and Dani Rodrik (professor, Harvard) are prominent detractors. Williamson himself believes the label has become hopelessly muddied, and appeals to the conspiratorially minded. If it now means "let's bash the state", he said, "we can all enjoy its wake".

Comments: The term has taken on a broader meaning, synonymous with neoliberalism and "market fundamentalism" foisted onto the Global South, rather than any discrete set of policy prescriptions. *The Economist* (magazine, British) has noted that those who say it is "a conspiracy to enrich bankers . . . are not entirely wrong".

The consensus: There's also a Beijing Consensus (a variant on the so-called "China Model"), a Buenos Aires Consensus, the Consensus on the Failures of the Washington Consensus, and something called the "Post-Washington Consensus Consensus". But no one can agree on what they mean either.